Reading and Writing for Today's Adults

Voyager 2

Deborah P. Adcock

Advisers to the Series

Mary Dunn Siedow
Director
North Carolina Literacy Resource Center
Raleigh, NC

Linda Thistlethwaite
Associate Director
The Central Illinois Adult Education Service Center
Western Illinois University
Macomb, IL

Reviewer

Joyce Clark
Instructor, Adult Basic Education
DeKalb Technical Institute
Adult Literacy Program
Clarkson, GA

New Readers Press

Acknowledgments

Carneiro, Isaura, adapted from WHERE THERE IS A WILL THERE IS A WAY. Reprinted by permission of St. Christopher House, 248 Ossington Ave., Toronto, Ontario, Canada

Farjeon, Eleanor. "The Quarrel" from Eleanor Farjeon's POEMS FOR CHILDREN originally appeared in OVER THE GARDEN WALL by Eleanor Farjeon. Copyright 1933, renewed 1961 by Eleanor Farjeon. Reprinted by permission of HarperCollins Publishers and David Higham Associates Ltd.

Hershenson, Miriam. "Husbands and Wives," by Miriam Hershenson. Published in SCOPE 1934. Copyright 1934. Reprinted (Reproduced) by permission of Scholastic Inc.

Leftwich, Joseph. "From Tomorrow On" translated by Joseph Leftwich. Reprinted from COMMENTARY, September 1951, by permission; all rights reserved.

Millay, Edna St. Vincent. "Lament" by Edna St. Vincent Millay from COLLECTED POEMS, HarperCollins. Copyright 1921, 1948 by Edna St. Vincent Millay. Used by permission of Elizabeth Barnett, literary executor.

Rodgers, Richard and Oscar Hammerstein II. "You've Got To Be Carefully Taught." Copyright © 1949 by Richard Rodgers and Oscar Hammerstein II. Copyright renewed. Williamson Music owner of publication and allied rights throughout the world. International copyright secured. Used by permission. All rights reserved.

Voyager: Reading and Writing for Today's Adults™ Voyager 2
ISBN 1-56420-152-X
Copyright © 1999
New Readers Press
Division of ProLiteracy Worldwide
1320 Jamesville Avenue, Syracuse, New York 13210

Printed in the United States of America
9 8 7 6 5 4 3

Director of Acquisitions and Development: Christina Jagger
Content Editor: Mary Hutchison
Photography: David Revette Photography, Inc.
Developer: Learning Unlimited, Oak Park, IL
Developmental Editor: Pamela Bliss
Contributing Writer: Betsy Rubin
Cover Designer: Gerald Russell
Designer: Kimbrly Koennecke
Copy Editor: Jeanna H. Walsh
Artist: Linda Alden
Illustrator: Cheri Bladholm

Contents

Introduction 5

Student Interest Inventory 6

Skills Preview 8

▼ **Unit 1: Family Ties** 13
Lesson 1 14
   Reading: "Family Is Family" 15
   Think About It: Understand Plot 18
   Write About It: Write a Sequence of Events 20
   Word Work: The Vowel Combinations *ie* and *ei* 21
Lesson 2 22
   Reading: "To My Son" 23
   Think About It: Understand the Main Idea and Details 26
   Write About It: Write a Letter 28
   Word Work: The Letter Combinations *ow* and *ou* 29
Lesson 3 30
   Reading: "The Quarrel" 31
   Think About It: Identify Rhythm and Rhyme 33
   Write About It: Write a Poem 35
Writing Skills Mini-Lesson: Adding Endings that Start with a Vowel 36
Unit 1 Review 37

▼ **Unit 2: Life Goes On** 39
Lesson 4 40
   Reading: "Saying Good-bye" 41
   Think About It: Understand Character 44
   Write About It: Write a Note 46
   Word Work: Context Clues 47
Lesson 5 48
   Reading: "Lament" 49
   Think About It: Understand the Use of Repetition 51
   Write About It: Write a Poem 53
Lesson 6 54
   Reading: "Life in the Hearing World" 55
   Think About It: Make Inferences 58
   Write About It: Write a Letter 60
   Word Work: Context Clues 61
Writing Skills Mini-Lesson: Using Capital Letters 62
Unit 2 Review 63

▼ **Unit 3: New Beginnings** 65
Lesson 7 66
   Reading: "Follow the Drinking Gourd" 67
   Think About It: Make Inferences 70
   Write About It: Write About a Song 71
Lesson 8 72
   Reading: "Al's Journal" 73
   Think About It: Understand the Main Idea and Details 76
   Write About It: Write a Journal Entry 78
   Word Work: Compound Words 79
Lesson 9 80
   Reading: "A New World" 81
   Think About It: Make Inferences 84
   Write About It: Conduct and Write an Interview 86
   Word Work: Prefixes and Roots 87
Writing Skills Mini-Lesson: Writing Sentences 88
Unit 3 Review 89

▼ **Unit 4: Celebrate Differences** 91
Lesson 10 92
   Reading: "Neighborly Celebrations" 93
   Think About It: Understand Plot and Character 96
   Write About It: Write a Description 98
   Word Work: Suffixes *-ful, -less, -able, -or* 99
Lesson 11 100
   Reading: "Celebrate an American Life" 101
   Think About It: Make Inferences 104
   Write About It: Write Your Autobiography 106
   Word Work: The Suffix *-ion* 107
Lesson 12 108
   Readings: "Manhattan"; "You've Got to Be Carefully Taught" 109
   Think About It: Identify Rhyme, Rhythm, and Repetition 112
   Write About It: Write a Poem 113
Writing Skills Mini-Lesson: Compound Sentences 114
Unit 4 Review 115

Skills Review 117

Answer Key 122

Reference Handbook 126
   Writing Skills 126
   The Writing Process 128

Introduction

Welcome to New Readers Press's *Voyager 2*. In this book, you will build your skills in reading and writing. You will improve your understanding of what you read. You will also work with your listening and speaking skills.

This book has four units. Each unit is based on a theme that reflects our day-to-day lives. In *Voyager 2,* you will be exploring these themes:

- ▶ Family Ties
- ▶ Life Goes On
- ▶ New Beginnings
- ▶ Celebrate Differences

Within each theme-based unit, you will find three lessons. Each lesson has the following features:

- ▶ **Before You Read:** a strategy to help you understand what you read
- ▶ **Key Words:** a preview of the harder words in the lesson
- ▶ **Reading:** a poem, story, biography, song, letter, or journal written by adults, for adults
- ▶ **After You Read:** questions and discussions about the reading
- ▶ **Think About It:** a reading skill that will help you understand what you read
- ▶ **Write About It:** an activity to improve your writing skills

Some lessons also have this feature:

- ▶ **Word Work:** strategies and skills to help you read and write better

We hope you enjoy exploring the themes and mastering the skills found in *Voyager 2*. We also invite you to continue your studies with the next book in our series, *Voyager 3.*

Student Interest Inventory

What is my educational goal?

_____

Check this side **BEFORE** you do this book.

Check this side **AFTER** you do this book.

a lot	a little	never	**When do I read?**	a lot	a little	never
			• by myself			
			• at my job			
			• at school			
			• with my children			
			• other:			

I can read these now.	I need help to read these.	I don't care to read these.	**What do I read?**	I can read these now.	I need help to read these.	I don't care to read these.
			• signs and labels			
			• instructions			
			• letters			
			• stories and poems			
			• newspapers			
			• magazines			
			• material for my job			
			• the Bible			
			• books to my children			
			• other books			
			• other:			

I am good at this.	I am improving at this.	I need to work on this.	**When I read, I can**	I am good at this.	I am improving at this.	I need to work on this.
			• figure out new words			
			• understand the main idea of what I read			
			• tell another person about what I read			

✔ Check this side **BEFORE** you do this book.　　✔ Check this side **AFTER** you do this book.

a lot	a little	never	When do I write?	a lot	a little	never
			• by myself			
			• at my job			
			• at school			
			• for my children			
			• other:			

I can do this now.	I need help to do this.	I don't care to do this.	What do I write or fill out?	I can do this now.	I need help to do this.	I don't care to do this.
			• lists			
			• notes and messages			
			• letters			
			• journal entries			
			• poems			
			• stories			
			• forms			
			• applications			
			• other:			

I am good at this.	I am improving at this.	I need help with this.	When I write, I can	I am good at this.	I am improving at this.	I need help with this.
			• think of good ideas			
			• organize my ideas			
			• express myself clearly so others understand what I mean			
			• write complete sentences			
			• capitalize words correctly			
			• use correct punctuation			

▶ Skills Preview

This preview will give you an idea of what you will do in this book. Before you begin Unit 1, complete as much of this preview as you can. Share your work with your instructor.

Reading Skills

Dear Dad,

I wish we could talk without getting mad. That is why I am writing to you. Last time we talked we both got angry. I said some things to you that I wished I had not said. I am sorry.

I know you do not agree with the choices I have made in my life. I know that you are unhappy with me. I do not do things to hurt you. I do them because I have to live my life the way I think is right.

Let's start all over again. Let's forget we said mean things to each other. Can you come to my place for dinner Friday? I still need you in my life. I need you to support me even if you do not agree with me.

Your loving daughter,
Jen

Choose the best answer to each question.

1. Who wrote the letter?
   (1) a father
   (2) a daughter

2. You can tell that Jen is the kind of person who
   (1) wants a better relationship with her father
   (2) will do what her father wants her to

3. What is the main idea of the letter?
   (1) Fathers and daughters should always agree with each other.
   (2) A daughter wants to start getting along with her father.

More Reading Skills

First Day ▬▬▬▬▬▬▬▬

Eva arrived at her new job on time. Her hands were shaking.
She felt the sweat on her forehead as she walked into the busy
office. "You can get right to work answering the phones," said
Eva's boss, Ms. Smiley. Ms. Smiley did not act very friendly.
In fact, she did not even smile once.

In the next few hours, many people passed by Eva's desk. Not
one of them said hello. No one even looked her way. Eva
began to wonder if she had made the right choice about taking
this job.

At noon, a woman came up to Eva's desk. "Hi, I'm Iris. Sorry
it's been so busy here. Most of the time things are not so
rushed and much more friendly. I'm taking my lunch now.
Would you like to join me?" Eva smiled. Maybe I made the
right choice after all, she thought.

Choose the best answer to each question.

4. How can you tell Eva is trying to be a responsible worker?
   (1) She will join Iris for lunch.
   (2) She got to work on time.

5. From the statements "Her hands were shaking. She felt the
   sweat on her forehead" you can tell that
   (1) Eva was nervous
   (2) Eva was hot

6. What is the turning point, or climax, of the story?
   (1) when no one stopped to say hello
   (2) when Iris is friendly to Eva

Write About It

On a separate piece of paper, write about the topic below. Use the checklist below to revise your draft.

Topic: Write about a problem you once had. Tell how you coped with the problem and perhaps how you solved it.

Revising Checklist

Revise your draft. Check that your draft

_____ includes your important ideas

_____ is clear and easy to read

_____ has details to explain what you mean

Make changes on your draft to improve your writing. Copy your revised draft of your writing on the lines below. Then share it with your instructor.

_____

_____

_____

_____

_____

_____

_____

_____

_____

_____

Skills Preview Answers

Reading Skills

1. (2)

2. (1)

3. (2)

More Reading Skills

4. (2)

5. (1)

6. (2)

Skills Chart

The questions in the Skills Preview assess students' familiarity with the following skills:

Question	Skill
1	finding details
2	understanding character
3	understanding main idea
4	understanding character
5	inferring
6	understanding plot

Unit 1 Family Ties

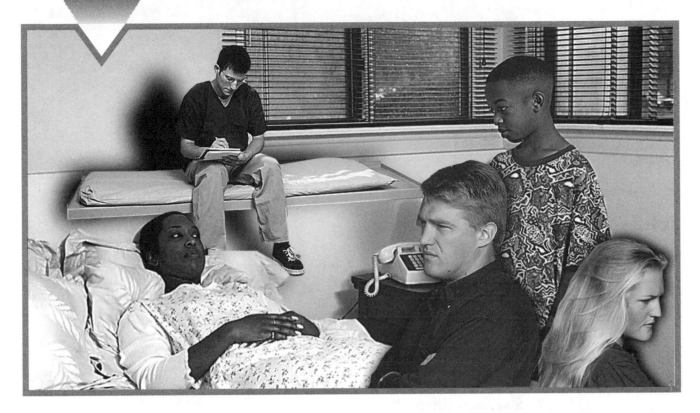

All families are different. Some families are large. Others are quite small. Some have many children. Others have none at all. But most families share one thing. They have family ties.

Family ties are the bonds that hold families together. They can be bonds of love. They can be bonds of trust and understanding. They also can be bonds of duty. These bonds are strong. They hold families together in good times and bad.

Before you read Unit 1, think of your own family. Do you have family ties? If so, how do they hold your family together?

▶ **Be an Active Reader**
As you read the selections in this unit
- Put a question mark (?) by things you do not understand.
- Underline words you do not know.

Lesson 1

LEARNING GOALS

Strategy: Imagine what you read
Reading: Read a story
Skill: Understand plot
Writing: Write a sequence of events
Word Work: The vowel combinations *ie* and *ei*

Before You Read

"Family Is Family" is a story about a woman who has been feeling sick for more than a month. Before you read "Family Is Family," think about a time when you felt very sick. What were you most worried about?

A. Imagine you are feeling sick. Place a check by each thing you might worry about.

_____ Do I have a serious illness?

_____ Will I lose time from work?

_____ Who will care for my family?

_____ Will doctors and tests cost me a lot of money?

B. Now imagine you are in the hospital. You cannot work. You need someone to take care of your child. Check each person who could help you.

_____ your husband or wife   _____ a friend

_____ your mother or father   _____ a neighbor

_____ another family member   _____ a church member

Key Words Read each sentence. Do you know the underlined words?

- The sick woman rode to the <u>hospital</u> in an <u>ambulance</u>.
- The doctor said she had an <u>ulcer</u> in her <u>stomach</u>.
- Marla felt <u>relief</u> when her mother came to help.

Family Is Family

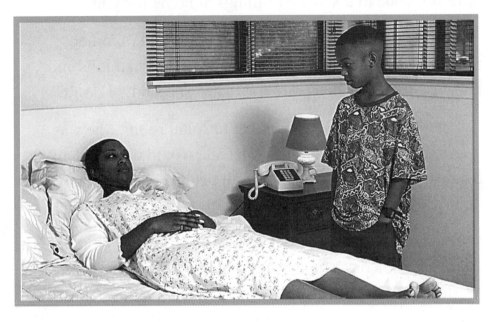

"Keith, I told you to go to bed!" Marla snapped at her 10-year-old son. Marla was tired. She felt sick. She did not mean to snap at Keith. But he was not listening to her.

Marla lay in bed with a burning pain in her stomach. She had felt it off and on for weeks. She knew it was a sign that something was wrong. But Marla did not have time to be sick. She had a son and a home to take care of. She had a job to go to.

"Besides," Marla thought, "if I'm sick, who will help me?" Marla knew she could not ask her mother. They had had a fight last year and had not spoken since. Marla felt all alone.

The next morning, Marla woke up at eight. When she stood up, a sharp pain shot through her stomach. She cried out and fell back onto the bed. Something was wrong.

Marla reached for the phone. She called an ambulance. She and Keith rode to the hospital. Keith was scared, and he cried.

Think about what you have read so far. Did you feel Marla's pain and picture her falling back? Could you see Keith's scared face and hear him cry?

◀ Check-in

After some tests, the doctor spoke with Marla. "You have an ulcer. You're going to be fine. But you will need to stay here at least overnight. Then you must rest at home. Do you have someone to take care of things at home for you?"

Marla shook her head. She could not ask her mother. She could not call her friends either. They all had jobs and families of their own to care for. "No," she said. "I don't."

Later that day, Marla lay in her hospital room. She was worried. Marla did not know what she would do. Suddenly, the door to her room opened. Keith peeked into the room. "I have a surprise for you, Mom," he said.

Keith opened the door wider. In walked Marla's mother, Ann. She smiled as she rushed to Marla's side. She gave Marla a big hug.

"How did you know?" asked Marla.

Ann looked over at Keith. "I have quite a grandson here," she said. "He called me and told me you were sick. I came right away. You and I may not always agree, but family is family. I will always be here for you."

Marla smiled with relief. She wasn't alone after all. In fact, she was starting to feel better already.

▶ Final Check-in

As you read the story, could you imagine how Marla felt when she was alone? Did you imagine how she looked when her mother came to help?

After You Read

A. Did the Story Make Sense? Reread sections you marked with a question mark (?). Do they make sense now? If not, discuss them with a partner or your instructor.

B. Build Your Vocabulary Look at the words you <u>underlined</u>. Can you figure them out now? If not, find out what they are. Add them to your word bank.

C. Answer These Questions

1. Choose one or more words to tell how Marla felt at the beginning and at the end of the story.

happy	worried	relieved
scared	alone	tense

   a. At the beginning, Marla felt _____

   b. At the end, she felt _____

2. Why did Marla feel she could not call her mother?
   (1) Her mother had never cared about her.
   (2) Her mother would still be angry about their fight.

3. What do you think will happen over the next few days?
   (1) Ann will take care of Keith.
   (2) Keith will stay in the hospital with Marla.

 Talk About It
Discuss the questions below with a partner or small group.
If you like, write a response.

Ann says, "Family is family." What is Ann telling her daughter?
Do you agree with Ann? Why or why not?

Think About It: Understand Plot

The **plot** of a story is what happens in the story. It is the action in the story. A plot follows a plan. The plan has three important parts. The parts usually take place in this order:

1. The **rising action** introduces the characters, the people in the story. It also tells about a problem or conflict.

2. The **climax** is the turning point of the story. It is the event that solves the problem. It usually happens near the end of the story.

3. The **falling action** tells the effects of the climax and draws the story to a close.

The plot of a story can be pictured like this:

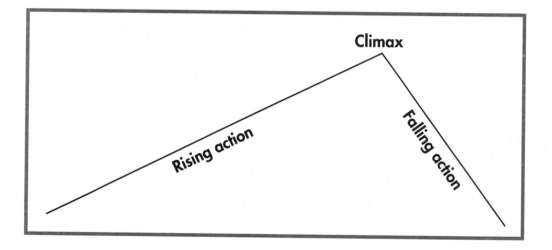

You can understand the plot of "Family Is Family" by answering three questions:

1. What is the main problem in the story?
    Marla is sick, and she is worried because she has no one to help her and her son.

All the events that take place when Marla is sick and worried are part of the rising action.

2. What event is the turning point?
   Suddenly the door opens. Marla's mother, Ann, has come to help.

This event is the climax. It helps solve Marla's problem.

3. What happens after the turning point?
   Ann explains how she learned Marla was sick. She says she will help
   Marla. Marla is relieved.

These events are the falling action.

Practice   Make a plot map of "Family Is Family." Write the answers to
the three questions on the correct lines below. You can make the
answers shorter if you like.

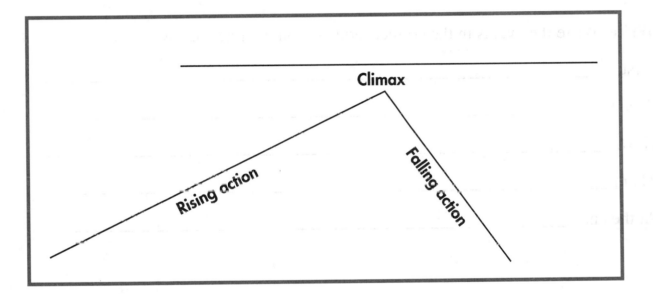

Retell   Retell the story in your own words. Use your plot map to help
you. Tell other details that you remember.

 Talk About It
   Discuss the questions below with a partner or small group.
   If you like, write a response.

   How is Keith part of Marla's problem? How is he part of the
   solution to her problem?

Write About It: Write a Sequence of Events

In a story, the **sequence of events** is the order in which the events happen. In "Family Is Family," you read about Marla and her family. Now write some of the events you read in the correct sequence. Some of the events in the story are listed below.

A. **Prewrite** Number these events in the order in which they happened.

_____ Ann appeared in Marla's room.

_____ Marla had a pain in her stomach.

_____ Keith called Ann.

_____ Marla smiled with relief.

_____ Marla went to the hospital.

B. **Write** Write the events in the correct sequence on the lines below.

First, _____

Second, _____

Next, _____

Then, _____

At the end, _____

Word Work: The Vowel Combinations *ie* and *ei*

The vowel combinations *ie* and *ei* can both make more than one sound.

A. Read the words below. Listen to the long vowel sound in each word.

ie as in *brief* (long *e*)		*ie* as in *pie* (long *i*)
chief	relief	die
field	belief	lie
piece	believe	tie

When you see *ie* in an unknown word longer than three letters, try long *e* first. When a three-letter word ends with *ie,* try long *i.*

B. Read these words. Listen to the long vowel sounds.

ei as in *eight* (long *a*)		*ei* as in *seize* (long *e*)	
neighbor	vein	ceiling	receive
weigh	veil	leisure	conceive
weight	rein	receipt	deceitful

When you see *eigh* in a word, try long *a*. When you see *cei,* try long *e.* When you see *ei* in a word, try long *a* first. If you don't recognize the word, try long *e.*

C. Read the words in each row. Cross out the word that does not have the same vowel sound as the first word.

1. belief	chief	tie	field
2. veil	freight	weight	receipt
3. ceiling	relief	sleigh	deceive
4. die	cries	pies	niece
5. eight	leisure	neighbor	weigh

Lesson 2

Strategy: Retell
Reading: Read a letter
Skill: Understand the main idea and details
Writing: Write a letter
Word Work: The letter combinations *ow* and *ou*

Before You Read

"To My Son" is a letter written by a man in prison. He is writing the letter to his young son. Before you read the letter, think about how a father in prison might feel. Check each thing you think he might want to tell his son.

_____ how many people live near the prison

_____ how he feels about not seeing his son

_____ how to write a letter

_____ what life in prison is like

_____ when the prison was built

_____ why he is in prison

_____ how much money the prison cost to build

Think about a time when you explained something to a child. What did you explain? What kind of words did you use? Were you able to make the child understand?

Key Words Read each sentence. Do you know the underlined words?

- This is a <u>special</u> place.
- A <u>correctional</u> <u>institution</u> is another name for a prison.
- My daily <u>schedule</u> includes a walk each morning.
- Lunch is served in the <u>cafeteria</u> at noon.

Use the Strategy
In this letter, you will read about a prisoner's thoughts and feelings. To help you understand the letter, keep asking yourself, "What is the writer telling about now?"

To My Son

Larry J.H.

Dear Son,

This is a special writing for you to help you understand why we cannot be together. At times you may feel angry at me. You may think that if I really loved you, I wouldn't have left you. I would have stayed at home.

So I want you to understand that I had to go away. I broke the law. That means that I did something I shouldn't have done. I had to go to court. The judge sent me to a special place called a correctional institution for men.

Check-in ▶ What has the father just told his son about?

This place is not like the jails they show on TV. We do have guards here but they do not carry guns.

All the men here live on a schedule, just as you do at home. We eat together in a big room like the cafeteria in a school. The food is okay. Every day, everyone goes to school or has a job to do. We can watch TV at night. The hardest part for me is that I cannot be with you.

Some kids think that if they had been better children, their fathers would have stayed at home. But this isn't true. You had nothing to do with the reason I had to come here. And there was nothing you could have done to change what happened to me. I'm here because of my own problems.

One father told me his child tried to get into trouble too, so he'd be sent here to be with him. But children cannot stay here. It made him sad to have his child get into trouble.

What is the father telling his son about now?

◀ **Check-in**

While I have to be away, I trust that you will do your best to get along well at school, at home, and in the neighborhood. I want you to have a good life now and in the future. Remember that the people taking care of you are doing it for you and me.

Someday I hope that you and I will talk about what happened to me. We will talk about how you felt and what you did while we had to be apart.

For now, let's be brave and strong. Please carry my love with you always.

Your father

▶ **Final Check-in**
Think about the letter you just read. Tell what the letter was about in your own words.

After You Read

A. Did the Letter Make Sense? Reread the sections you marked with a question mark (?). Do they make sense now? If not, discuss them with a partner or your instructor.

B. Build Your Vocabulary Look at the words you <u>underlined</u>. Can you figure them out now? If not, find out what they are. Add them to your word bank.

C. Answer These Questions

1. Check each thing that the father talked about in his letter.

   _____ what the prison looks like

   _____ why he is in prison

   _____ what life in prison is like

   _____ how his being in prison was not his son's fault

   _____ how to do well in school

   _____ what he wants his son to do

2. Which title would be better for this letter?
   (1) A Prisoner Leads a Hard Life
   (2) A Father Writes a Difficult Letter

3. How do you think the father feels about his son?

   _____

   _____

 Talk About It

Discuss the questions below with a partner or small group.
If you like, write a response.

The father writes, "Someday I hope that you and I will talk about what happened to me. We will talk about how you felt." Do you think the father and child should talk about what happened? Why or why not? What do you think the child might tell his father?

Think About It: Understand the Main Idea and Details

The **main idea** of a piece of writing is the most important point that the writer wants to share. **Supporting details** help explain the main idea.

Think about the letter "To My Son." Think about the most important point in the letter. Sometimes the main idea is stated by the author. Sometimes you have to put it in your own words. The main idea of the letter is this:

- A father in prison wants his son to know he loves him.

These are some details in the letter that support the main idea:

- The hardest part of prison life is that the father cannot be with his son.
- The father wants his son to know that his son is not to blame.
- The father says, "Please carry my love with you always."

Which of these details in the letter also supports, or helps explain, the main idea?

(1) The father lives on a schedule, as the son does.
(2) The father wants his son to have a good life.

The second detail helps show you the father's love for his son. It supports the main idea.

You can picture the main idea and details this way:

Main Idea			
A father in prison wants his son to know he loves him.			
Detail	**Detail**	**Detail**	**Detail**
The hardest part of prison life is that the father cannot be with his son.	The father wants his son to know that his son is not to blame.	The father says, "Please carry my love with you always."	The father wants his son to have a good life.

Practice   Read the story below. Think about the main idea of the story.

A Day Together

   Fred is going to spend the day with his son. They have their
day all planned. First, they are going on a bike ride. Then they
are going to stop for lunch. Later, they are going to watch a
ball game. In the evening, they plan to see a movie.

1.   Which of the following tells the main idea of "A Day Together"?
     (1) Fred and his son are going to the movies.
     (2) Fred has plans to spend the day with his son.
     (3) Fred and his son are going to watch the ball game.

2.   Write the main idea of the story "A Day Together" in the chart below.
     Then write four details that help support the main idea.

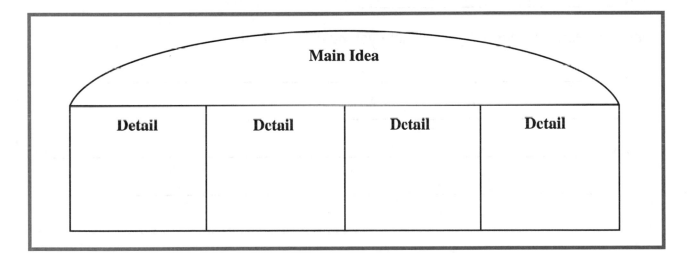

3.   Share your completed chart with a partner. Compare the ideas in both
     your charts.

Write About It: Write a Letter

In "To My Son," a father gave advice to his child. Now write a letter with advice you would give a child in your family. The child could even be you when you were young.

A. Prewrite Think of what you have learned about life that you would like to tell a child. List three things you think would help a child have a good life.

_____

_____

_____

B. Write Now write your letter on the lines below.

Dear _____,

Here are some things I think will help you have a good life.

First, _____

_____

Second, _____

_____

Third, _____

_____

I hope you find these things good to know.

With love,

_____

▶ **Hold on to this work.** You may use it again at the end of this unit.

Word Work: The Letter Combinations *ow* and *ou*

A. The letter combination *ow* makes more than one sound. Read the words below. Listen to the vowel sound in each word.

ow as in *low*		*ow* as in *now*	
blow	own	how	down
grow	shown	allow	clown
know	tomorrow	crowd	shower

When you see *ow* in an unknown word, try long *o* first.

B. The vowel combination *ou* makes many different sounds. Listen to the vowel sounds in the words below.

ou as in *out*		*ou* as in *young*		*ou* as in *could*	
about	mouth	double	rough	could	couldn't
loud	around	touch	tough	would	wouldn't
house	county	country	enough	should	shouldn't

ou as in *you*	*ou* as in *soul*	*our* as in *four*	*ou* as in *ought*
soup	dough	pour	bought
group	shoulder	your	brought
youth	though	court	fought
through	thorough	mourn	thought

When you see *ou* in an unknown word, try *ou* as in *out* first. It is the most common sound for *ou*.

C. Read the words in each row. Cross out the word that does not have the same vowel sound as the first word.

1. show	now	blow	crow
2. plow	cow	mow	brow
3. group	soup	youth	though
4. young	rough	double	mouth
5. about	loud	touch	shout

Lesson 3

LEARNING GOALS

Strategy: Use your experience to help you understand what you read
Reading: Read a poem
Skill: Identify rhythm and rhyme
Writing: Write a poem

Before You Read

"The Quarrel" is a poem about a fight a brother and sister had over something unimportant. Before you read "The Quarrel," think about a foolish fight you had with someone in your family.

A. Who did you have the fight with?

_____

What was the fight about?

_____

When did you see that the fight was foolish?

_____

What did you do then?

_____

B. Now think of what you know about poetry. Check each thing you might expect to find in a poem.

_____ a table of contents   _____ short lines

_____ a title   _____ long speeches

_____ words that rhyme   _____ a beat or rhythm

Key Words Read each sentence. Do you know the underlined words?
- I <u>quarreled</u> with my brother over something foolish.
- There was only a <u>slight</u> hurt to her feelings.
- He <u>thumped</u> me on the back with his hand.

▶ **Use the Strategy**

To help you understand "The Quarrel," ask yourself, "Has something like this ever happened to me?"

The Quarrel

Eleanor Farjeon

I quarreled with my brother,
I don't know what about,
One thing led to another
And somehow we fell out.
The start of it was slight,
The end of it was strong,
He said he was right,
I knew he was wrong!

We hated one another.
The afternoon turned black
Then suddenly my brother
Thumped me on the back,
And said, "Oh, *come* along!
We can't go on all night—
I was in the wrong."
So he was in the right.

▶ **Check-in**

How is what happened in the poem like your own experience? How is it different?

After You Read

A. Did the Poem Make Sense? Reread sections you marked with a question mark (?). Do they make sense now? If not, discuss them with a partner or your instructor.

B. Build Your Vocabulary Look at the words you <u>underlined</u>. Can you figure them out now? If not, find out what they are. Add them to your word bank.

C. Answer These Questions

1. Think about a foolish quarrel you had with someone. How did you feel afterward? Check the answers that are true for you. Add another feeling if you like.

   _____ upset

   _____ worried

   _____ foolish

   _____

2. The brother said, "I was in the wrong." What does the poet mean by then saying, "So he was in the right"?
   (1) The brother really had been wrong.
   (2) The brother was right to end the fight.

3. "The start of it was slight, The end of it was strong." What do these lines mean?
   (1) The fight started off small, then became worse.
   (2) The brother was not angry, but the sister was.

▶ **Talk About It**
Discuss the questions below with a partner or small group. If you like, write a response.

Why do we fight with people in our families? Why is it important to make up?

Think About It: Identify Rhythm and Rhyme

Rhythm

Poems contain a **rhythm,** or beat. The rhythm is created because certain words and word parts are stressed. For example, the capital letters show the stresses in the first line of "The Quarrel."

i QUARreled with my BROTHer.

The stresses form a pattern through the poem. This pattern is the rhythm. Read "The Quarrel" out loud. Listen to the rhythm as you read. Clap or tap the rhythm as you read it aloud again.

Rhyme

Many poems also contain words that **rhyme.** When two words rhyme, they end with the same sound. For example, *blow* and *show* rhyme.

Most rhymes are at the ends of the lines in a poem. Look at the ends of the first few lines in "The Quarrel." What word rhymes with *brother?*

_____

The word at the end of the third line, *another*, rhymes with *brother*.

A. Read the first part of "The Quarrel" out loud again. Write the word in the poem that rhymes with each word below.

about _____

slight _____

strong _____

Did you write that *out* rhymes with *about*, *right* rhymes with *slight*, and *wrong* rhymes with *strong?*

B. Read aloud the second part of the poem. Write the word pairs that rhyme.

_____   _____

_____   _____

_____   _____

_____   _____

The rhyming pairs are: *another* and *brother; black* and *back; along* and *wrong; night* and *right.*

Words that rhyme do not have to be spelled alike. For example, *rain* and *cane* rhyme. Also, words that are spelled alike but sound different are not rhyming words. As we saw in lesson 2, *low* and *now* do not rhyme.

Practice

A. Read the words in each row. Cross out the word that does not rhyme with the other words.

1. tie	try	lie	cried
2. rain	weigh	rein	vein
3. blow	grow	allow	know
4. down	shown	town	clown
5. bought	thought	about	ought
6. rough	stuff	though	tough

B. Write a word that rhymes with each word below. Remember, words that rhyme do not have to be spelled alike.

1. sky _____   6. four _____

2. brief _____   7. blow _____

3. eight _____   8. how _____

4. out _____   9. weigh _____

5. round _____   10. through _____

Write About It: Write a Poem

In "The Quarrel," you read about a foolish fight between a brother and a sister. Now write your own poem about a family member. It could be about a foolish fight, or it could be about anything in your life with this family member. You can use the poem started below if you like.

A. Prewrite Think about the family member you want to write about. Read the lines of the poem below. On another paper, jot down different ways to complete each line.

Remember that not all poems have rhyme or a regular rhythm. Decide if you want yours to.

B. Write Use your best ideas to finish this poem.

My _____
         (family member)

Sometimes we fight about _____

Sometimes we laugh about _____

Sometimes we cry about _____

Always we _____

▶ **Hold on to this work.** You may use it again at the end of this unit.

 Talk About It
Share your poem with a partner. Tell what you liked about your partner's poem. Ask what your partner liked about yours.

Writing Skills Mini-Lesson

Adding Endings that Start with a Vowel

Sometimes you need to add an ending to a word. When the ending starts with a vowel, follow these spelling rules:

1. **For most words, just add the ending.**
    look + ing = looking   play + er = player   assist + ant = assistant

2. **If a one-syllable word ends with one vowel plus one consonant, double the final consonant (unless it is *w* or *x*).**
    drop + ed = dropped   hid + en = hidden   **but:** fix + ed = fixed

3. **If a word ends with a silent *e*, drop the *e*.**
    type + ist = typist   use + able = usable   operate + or = operator

4. **If a word ends with a consonant plus *y*, change the *y* to *i* unless the ending starts with *i*.**
    happy + est = happiest   carry + er = carrier   **but:** carry + ing = carrying

Practice Copy the paragraph below on your own paper. Add the endings to the words as indicated. You may have to add, drop, or change letters. Then read the paragraph.

   Last night, my family was relax (+ ing) and play (+ ing) cards with my two aunts. Suddenly my old (+ er) aunt announce (+ ed), "Luis and I are get (+ ing) marry (+ ed). My mother hug (+ ed) her, cry (+ ing), "Finally! I never stop (+ ed) hope (+ ing)! You'll be the happy (+ est) couple." Then all of us start (+ ed) plan (+ ing) the wedding.

Unit 1 Review

Reading Review

This reading is about family ties. Read it and answer the questions.

Grandma Pat

Lately I have been thinking of Grandma Pat. When I was a boy, I spent a lot of time at Grandma Pat's. She cooked me dinner when my mom and dad were working. And she told me the best stories. I could listen to her stories all day.

When I grew older, I would visit her. She was always glad to see me. When I had a problem, Grandma Pat would understand. "Sit down. Tell me what is bothering you," she would say. We would sit in her kitchen. I would talk and she would listen. She acted as if she would listen all day.

Now I know how lucky I was to have Grandma Pat. She was someone who always cared for me. She was someone I could tell my secrets to. Most of all, she made me feel like someone special.

Today I look at my little granddaughter. She is only two months old. But I promise her one thing. I will always try to be there for her—the way Grandma Pat was there for me.

Choose the best answer for each question.

1. Which of the following tells the main idea of the reading?
   (1) The writer was lucky to have Grandma Pat when he was young.
   (2) Grandma Pat didn't care much about the writer.

2. Which of the following details helps support the main idea?
   (1) The writer's granddaughter is two months old.
   (2) Grandma Pat made the writer feel special.

3. Which would be a good title for this piece of writing?
   (1) My Grandma Pat
   (2) It's Hard to Be a Grandparent

Writing Process

In Unit 1, you wrote two first drafts. Choose the draft that you would like to work with more. You will revise, edit, and make a final copy of this draft.

＿＿＿＿ your letter of advice to a child (page 28)

＿＿＿＿ your poem about a family member (page 35)

Find the first draft you chose. Then turn to page 128 in this book. Follow steps 3, 4, and 5 in the Writing Process to create a final draft.

As you revise, check for this specific point:

Letter: Are there three clear pieces of advice in your letter?
Poem: Did you include your best ideas to tell about you and your family member?

Unit 2   Life Goes On

Sometimes things happen in life that cause us pain or sorrow. At one time or another, each of us faces a crisis. It could be a health problem. It could be trouble at home or on the job. It could be your best friend moving away. It could even be the death of a loved one.

We have to learn to cope with things that we cannot change. There are different ways of coping. We may make new friends. We may learn to do things differently. Or we may simply have to learn to live with a loss. We learn that life goes on in spite of our pain or sorrow.

Before you start Unit 2, think about a crisis in your own life. How did you cope with it? What helped you most?

 Be an Active Reader

As you read the selections in this unit
- Put a question mark (?) by things you do not understand.
- Underline words you do not know. Try to use context clues to figure them out.

Lesson 4

LEARNING GOALS

Strategy: Imagine what you read
Reading: Read a story
Skill: Understand character
Writing: Write a note
Word Work: Context clues

Before You Read

"Saying Good-bye" is a story about two women. They are best friends. Think about the title. What do you think might happen in the story?

_____

_____

A. Have you ever had to say good-bye to a good friend? How does saying good-bye make you feel? Check each way you might feel. Add some feelings of your own if you like.

_____ angry   _____ upset   _____

_____ sad   _____ bored   _____

B. Now check each thing that might be helpful to do when you have to say good-bye to a friend.

_____ forget the friend as soon as you can

_____ keep in touch with the friend

_____ try to make new friends

_____ pretend you don't care

Key Words Read the sentence. Do you know the underlined word?

• Hector had an <u>interview</u> for a new job last week.

Use the Strategy

To help you understand this story, imagine you can see and hear what is happening. Picture the people in the story. Hear what they say. Imagine how they must be feeling.

Saying Good-bye

Rosa and Carmen sat in the cafeteria eating lunch. They had been best friends since high school. Now they worked in the same big store. They ate lunch together every day.

Rosa and Carmen were close. But they were very different. Carmen loved people. Carmen had a husband, Hector, and a young son. Rosa was quiet. Carmen was her only close friend. Rosa's family had moved back to Mexico. Since her boyfriend, Manny, left, she had lived on her own.

Rosa could read Carmen like a book. She could tell what mood Carmen was in. Today Carmen seemed quiet. And it was not because of the noise in the cafeteria. Rosa said, "Carmen, what's wrong with you? You seem down."

Check-in ▶ Try to picture the cafeteria and hear the noise. Imagine Rosa and Carmen sitting together. How do they look?

Carmen looked at Rosa. She said, "I have something to tell you. You know Hector finished night school. Well, he had a job interview a few weeks ago. Yesterday, he got the job. But it's in L.A. We have to move there."

Lesson 4 **41** ◀

Rosa's stomach turned. Los Angeles was 200 miles away. If Carmen moved, Rosa would be all alone.

Rosa tried to stay calm. She did not want Carmen to know how scared she felt. Because she was so quiet, people thought nothing ever bothered her. But that was not true. It was just hard for Rosa to show her feelings.

How do you imagine Rosa looks now? How does she feel?

◀ **Check-in**

Carmen kept talking. "I'll miss you. When my mother died, you knew just what to say and do. When my nylons ran on my wedding day, you gave me your own! And when I found out I was pregnant, you were the first person I told."

Rosa took Carmen's hand. She did not tell Carmen how alone she would feel. Instead, Rosa said, "Carmen, I'm happy for you and Hector. He's worked hard to get a good job. The two of you will love L.A. And you know I'll always be here for you."

Carmen smiled. "You always did know the right thing to say." Then she saw the clock on the wall. "Oh, I've got to go. Are you coming too?" she asked.

"No, I've got a few more minutes," Rosa answered. "I want to finish my coffee." But when Carmen had gone, Rosa went into the ladies' room. She looked in the mirror. There she saw a young woman with short black hair and large worried eyes.

Then Rosa reminded herself. She had made it through when her family moved. She had made it through when Manny left. She could make it through saying good-bye to Carmen. Besides, she did not really have to say good-bye. Two hundred miles isn't so far. And there is always the phone.

▶ **Final Check-in**

Could you picture what happened in the story? Could you hear the friends talking and imagine how they were feeling?

After You Read

A. Did the Story Make Sense? Reread sections you marked with a question mark (?). Do they make sense now? If not, discuss them with a partner or your instructor.

B. Build Your Vocabulary Look at the words you <u>underlined</u>. Can you figure them out now? If not, find out what they are. Add them to your word bank.

C. Answer These Questions

1. What did Rosa see when she looked in the mirror?

(1) 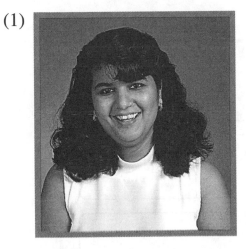 (2)

2. What is Rosa's main problem in the story?
   (1) She did not have a boyfriend.
   (2) Her only friend was moving away.

3. What does the last line of the story mean?
   (1) Rosa could talk with Carmen on the phone.
   (2) A new friend might call Rosa.

 Talk About It

Discuss the questions below with a partner or small group.
If you like, write a response.

Why didn't Rosa tell Carmen how she really felt? Do you think Rosa did the right thing when she did not tell Carmen how she was feeling? Why or why not?

Think About It: Understand Character

A **character** is a person in a story. As you read a story, you can learn things about the characters. For example, you may learn

- what a character looks like
- how the character deals with life
- the character's background
- what the character thinks
- what kind of person the character is

For example, this character web shows some things you learned about Carmen in "Saying Good-bye":

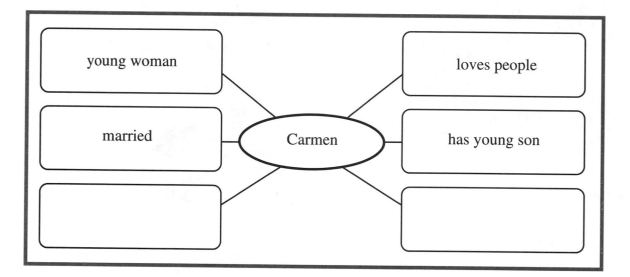

Fill in the rest of the character web with two other things you learned about Carmen. Choose from this list.

dresses in bright clothes	is moving
Rosa's best friend	is usually late
has a sense of humor	is often angry

The story says Carmen is moving. It also tells you that Carmen and Rosa are best friends. Those two phrases complete the character web of Carmen.

Practice

The **main character** is the person that the story is mostly about. Rosa is the main character in "Saying Good-bye."

1. Make a list of words or phrases that describe Rosa. Describe the kind of person she is as well as the way she looks. Look back at the story if you like. The first one is done for you.

   <u>Mexican background</u>   _____

   _____   _____

   _____   _____

2. Make a character web about Rosa. Write her name in the large oval in the center. Then use your list from number 1 to complete the web.

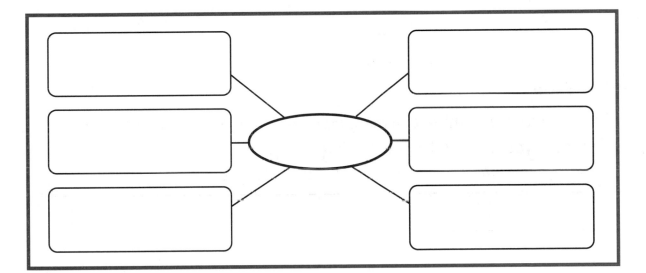

3. Which statement would Rosa probably agree with?
   (1) Grin and bear it.
   (2) Don't hold anything back.

4. Write one way that Rosa and Carmen are alike.

   _____

5. Write one way that they are different.

   _____

Write About It: Write a Note

In "Saying Good-bye," you read about Rosa. Her best friend was moving away. Suppose you were to write a note to Rosa. You want to help her feel better. Suggest some ways to cope with Carmen's moving away.

A. Prewrite Review the character web you made for Rosa. On these lines, list a few ideas you would say to her in a note.

_____   _____

_____   _____

_____   _____

B. Write Use your ideas to write your note. The note has been started for you.

_____

(date)

Dear Rosa,

    I know you must miss Carmen. Here are some things that might help you cope with her moving away.

_____

_____

_____

_____

_____

Sincerely,

_____

▶ **Hold on to this work.** You may use it again at the end of this unit.

Word Work: Context Clues

How can you figure out a word you don't know when you are reading? One way is to look at the words and sentences around it for hints. These hints are called **context clues.** Read these sentences. Imagine the blank is a word you can't read.

- Hector was looking for work. A few weeks ago, he had a job

  _____. Yesterday, he got the job.

How can you figure out the word that goes in the blank? A hint in the first sentence is "looking for work." In the last sentence, a hint is "got the job." What do people do between looking for work and getting a job?

_____

People looking for work go on job interviews. Put the word *interview* in the blank. Read the sentences. Does *interview* make sense? Do you think *interview* is the missing word? Probably it is.

When you read, use context clues to figure out words.

Practice Some words are missing in the sentences below. Use context clues and the first letter of each word to figure out what the word is. Write it on the line.

1. When Carmen left, Rosa ate alone in the c_____.

2. Rosa was b_____ by the fact that Carmen was moving. But she acted happy for Carmen instead of upset.

3. Rosa looked in the bathroom m_____ before she went back to work.

Lesson 5

LEARNING GOALS

Strategy: Use what you know to understand what you read
Reading: Read two poems
Skill: Understand the use of repetition
Writing: Write a poem

Before You Read

In this lesson, you will read a poem called "Lament." A lament is a song or poem that tells of grief or sorrow. The poem "Lament" tells about a woman who is coping with the death of her husband.

In Lesson 3, you read a poem, "The Quarrel," that had rhyme and a strong rhythm. "Lament" does not have rhyme or a regular rhythm. Instead, the woman in the poem speaks in a more natural way.

Think of how it feels when a loved one dies. Check each word below that tells how the woman in the poem might feel. Add other words if you like.

_____ sorry   _____ peaceful   _____

_____ sad   _____ depressed   _____

Key Words Read each sentence. Do you know the underlined words?
- The <u>medicine</u> made Dan feel better.
- The man was wearing gray <u>trousers</u>.

▶ **48** Unit 2 Life Goes On

Use the Strategy

To help you understand the poem "Lament," think about what a woman must do after her husband has died. What does she say to her children? How does she probably feel?

Lament

Edna St. Vincent Millay

Listen, children:
Your father is dead.
From his old coats
I'll make you little jackets;
I'll make you little trousers
From his old pants.
There'll be in his pockets
Things he used to put there,
Keys and pennies
Covered with tobacco;
Dan shall have the pennies
To save in his bank;
Anne shall have the keys
To make a pretty noise with.
Life must go on,
And the dead be forgotten;
Life must go on,
Though good men die;
Anne, eat your breakfast;
Dan, take your medicine;
Life must go on;
I forget just why.

▶ **Check-in**

As you read the poem, did you think about what a widow must do? Did the actions and thoughts of the speaker make sense? Did she feel the way you thought she would?

After You Read

A. Did the Poem Make Sense? Reread sections you marked with a question mark (?). Do they make sense now? If not, discuss them with a partner or your instructor.

B. Build Your Vocabulary Look at the words you <u>underlined</u>. Can you figure them out now? If not, find out what they are. Add them to your word bank.

C. Answer These Questions

1. How did the woman in the poem feel?

_____

2. Compare your answer with the words you checked on page 48. Did the woman's feeling surprise you? _____

3. Who is the woman talking to?
   (1) friends of the family
   (2) her two children

4. What is the woman's main concern in the poem?
   (1) forgetting her husband
   (2) getting on with everyday matters

 Talk About It

Discuss the questions below with a partner or small group. If you like, write a response.

How is the woman in "Lament" coping with the death of her husband? What does she mean by the last line: "I forget just why"?

Think About It: Understand the Use of Repetition

Poets choose their words carefully. Often they will repeat a word or phrase two or more times. This **repetition** helps poets get their meaning across.

Read aloud the poem "Lament." Write the statement that is repeated three times.

_____

The statement "Life must go on" means the family must keep on with their lives. The woman repeats it three times because she is trying to make herself accept it. But each time she repeats the statement, it is followed by a different line. The three different lines help you understand her true meaning:

> 1. ▶ Life must go on,
>   And the dead be forgotten;

When the woman speaks these lines, she is trying to convince herself that she cannot spend all her time thinking about her husband. She must go on with her life and care for her children.

> 2. ▶ Life must go on,
>   Though good men die;

The woman is trying to accept that goodness does not spare a person from death. Perhaps she thinks that if she repeats the phrase "Life must go on" enough times, she will believe it.

> 3. ▶ Life must go on;
>   I forget just why.

Repeating "Life must go on" has not yet convinced her of its truth. She is still having a hard time accepting her husband's death and the fact that she must go on without him. At this moment, she is feeling that life is empty and without meaning.

Practice

During World War II, the leaders of Nazi Germany sent many Jewish people and others to concentration camps. Millions of those people died in the camps. The camps became known as death camps. The following poem was written by a child in one such camp.

Think about what life could have been like for the child who wrote this poem. As you read it, look for a repeated phrase that helps you understand his message.

From Tomorrow On

From tomorrow on I shall be sad,
From tomorrow on.
Not today. Today I shall be glad.
And every day, no matter how bitter it may be,
I shall say:
From tomorrow on I shall be sad,
Not today.

THE BETTMANN ARCHIVE

1. Write·the three-word phrase that is repeated three times in the poem.

   _____

2. What is the poet "putting off" until tomorrow?

   _____

3. When you keep "putting something off" until tomorrow, do you ever do it? Explain.

   _____

4. What is the poet's main message?
   (1) He believes he will be free tomorrow.
   (2) By coping with his situation one day at a time, he keeps his will to live.

Write About It: Write a Poem

In this lesson, you read two poems. Both poets wrote about coping. Both poems showed how poets repeat a phrase to help you understand their message. Now write a poem of your own.

A. **Prewrite** Think about something you would like to change about yourself or your life. What could you do to change it? Write down a few ideas on a separate paper.

B. **Write** Complete the poem below with your own ideas.

From Today On ▬▬▬▬▬▬▬▬▬

by _____

From today on _____,

From today on.

Today I shall _____.

And every day, no matter how _____,

I shall say:

From today on _____.

▶ **Hold on to this work.** You may use it again at the end of this unit.

> ▶ **Talk About It**
> Discuss these questions with a partner or small group.
> If you like, write a response.
>
> How is the poet of "From Tomorrow On" coping with life in a concentration camp? How does his way of coping contrast with that of the woman in the poem "Lament"?

Lesson 6

LEARNING GOALS

Strategy: Retell
Reading: Read a biography
Skill: Make inferences
Writing: Write a letter
Word Work: Context clues

Before You Read

"Life in the Hearing World" is a biography of Michael Delani. A biography is a true story about the life of a real person. Michael is a young man who is deaf.

A. Here is one fact you might find out about a person in a biography. What are some other things?

___When the person was born___   _____

_____   _____

B. What other things might you read about in a biography about a young deaf person? Check each answer you think is true.

_____ what life without being able to hear is like

_____ the number of deaf people in the world

_____ how the person copes with being deaf

_____ all the different causes of deafness

Key Words Read each sentence. Do you know the underlined words?

- Doctors were not sure the sick child would <u>survive</u>.
- Use your hands and arms to <u>communicate</u> in <u>sign language</u>.
- Deaf people like Michael are <u>physically</u> <u>challenged</u>.

Life in the Hearing World

MICHAEL DELANI

When Michael Delani was born, he had a weak heart. He also was born without the part of the body that brings food down to the stomach. "We can try to help your son," a doctor told Michael's parents. "But we are not sure he will survive."

Michael did survive. But by the age of 3, Michael still could not speak. Then his parents learned their son was deaf.

Deafness did not stop Michael. He went to a school for deaf children. He learned to read, write, and do math. He and his family learned sign language. Michael also began to learn how to speak.

While at school, Michael got a hearing-ear dog named Prince. A hearing-ear dog is trained to act as the ears of a deaf person. Prince would alert Michael when he heard the alarm clock, the doorbell, or a fire alarm. Michael and Prince soon became best friends.

Check-in ▶ Think about what you have already read. What facts have you learned about Michael? What has he done to cope with living in the hearing world?

Michael tried to live his life like other young people. He learned how to drive. After he finished school, he looked for a job. "I want to earn my own money," he said.

But Michael had a hard time getting a job. Michael could speak, but his words were hard to understand. Employers had a hard time interviewing him. So he had his parents go with him. They explained to employers what he said. Michael finally got a job as a cook.

When Michael was in his 20s, Prince died. Michael decided he did not need another hearing-ear dog. A few years later, Michael made another big decision. "I want my own apartment," he told his family.

What else has happened to Michael? What other things has he done to cope with living in the hearing world?

◀ **Check-in**

Michael's parents were not sure living on his own was a good idea. "Have you thought about how hard it might be?" they asked. "How will you know if someone is at your door? What if there is a fire?"

Still, Michael's family helped him look for a place to live. One day, he learned about a great apartment in another town. The apartment building was set up for the deaf and other physically challenged people. For deaf people, a light in their apartment would flash if someone was at the door. In case of fire, lights would flash in each room. The bed would shake too. And Michael would have a teletypewriter, or TTY. A TTY is a special typewriter hooked up to a telephone. A person types a message and sends it over the telephone to someone else with a TTY who reads the message and types a response.

Michael moved into the apartment there. He now lives on his own. Every day brings new challenges. But Michael is happy. He is enjoying this latest chapter in his life.

▶ **Final Check-in**

Were you able to keep track of the main events in Michael's life?

After You Read

A. Did the Biography Make Sense? Reread sections you marked with a question mark (?). Do they make sense now? If not, discuss them with a partner or your instructor.

B. Build Your Vocabulary Look at the words you <u>underlined</u>. Can you figure them out now? If not, find out what they are. Add them to your word bank.

C. Answer These Questions

1. List three important things you would tell someone about Michael Delani.

   _____

   _____

   _____

2. Give an example of how each of the following helped Michael to cope in the hearing world:

   a. his parents _____

   b. an animal _____

   c. a machine _____

3. If Michael were looking for a store and could not find it, what would he probably do?
   (1) ask someone for directions in writing
   (2) go home and forget about shopping

 Talk About It
With a partner or small group, retell Michael's story in your own words. Then listen as your partner retells the story. Did both you and your partner include the same facts?

Think About It: Make Inferences

When you infer, you use clues to figure out something that is not actually stated—you "read between the lines." You **make inferences** every time you use your knowledge and experience and "put two and two together" to make sense of what you see and hear. For instance, if you see a friend carrying bags of groceries, you can infer that he has been grocery shopping. You can infer facts and ideas when you read. For example, read the two sentences from "Life in the Hearing World" below.

- "We can try to help your son," a doctor told Michael's parents. "But we are not sure he will survive."

Were Michael's health problems serious? _____

Those two sentences do not tell you everything about Michael's health. But you can infer that his problems were very serious. If Michael's problems were minor, the doctors would not have told his parents that he might not survive.

You can infer things about characters as you read. To do so, look at how they act and what they say. For example, look at Michael's parents. You read that they

- learned sign language with him
- helped him get a job
- worried about him moving out
- helped him find an apartment

Which would you infer about Michael's parents?
(1) They thought he was a burden.
(2) They cared about him very much.

His parents' actions showed they cared about Michael. The biography never directly stated that they cared about Michael. But you could infer it.

Practice

Read the information from "Life in the Hearing World." Then use it to infer the answer to each question.

▶ When Michael Delani was born, he had a weak heart. He also was born without the part of the body that brings food down to the stomach. "We can try to help your son," a doctor told Michael's parents. "But we are not sure he will survive."

Michael did survive.

1. Were the doctors able to help Michael? _____

▶ But Michael had a hard time getting a job. Michael could speak, but his words were hard to understand. Employers had a hard time interviewing him. So he had his parents go with him. They explained to employers what he said. Michael finally got a job as a cook.

2. How long did it take Michael to find a job?
    (1) quite a while
    (2) a few days

▶ When Michael was in his 20s, Prince died. Michael decided he did not need another hearing-ear dog. A few years later, Michael made another big decision. "I want my own apartment," he told his family.

3. Think about the way Michael acted and the things he said.
    What kind of person can you infer he is?
    (1) He is shy and feels sorry for himself.
    (2) He is determined to be independent.

Write About It: Write a Letter

In "Life in the Hearing World," you learned about Michael Delani.
Now write a letter to Michael asking other things you would like to
learn about him.

A. Prewrite Think of five more things you'd like to know about Michael.
Think of five questions to ask him. List the best three questions here.

_____

_____

_____

B. Write Finish this letter with your questions.

_____

(date)

Dear Michael,

I have read about your life. I'd like to learn more about you. Here are
some questions I have.

_____

_____

_____

_____

Sincerely,

_____

▶ **Hold on to this work.** You may use it again at the end of this unit.

Word Work: Context Clues

As we saw in Lesson 4, **context clues** are hints in sentences that you can use to understand new words. They can help you figure out words you do not know. They can also help you figure out meanings you are not sure of.

For example, suppose you did not know what "physically challenged" meant in this sentence:

 The apartment building was set up for deaf and other physically challenged people.

The context clues are "deaf and other . . . people." Deaf people are examples of people who are physically challenged. So you can figure out that "physically challenged" describes people who have challenging problems with their bodies.

Practice Use context clues in each sentence to choose the meaning of the underlined word.

1. Michael's <u>employer</u> explained the job of cook to him.
   (1) person who hires workers
   (2) person who likes to talk

2. Michael's bed shook to <u>alert</u> him that there was a fire.
   (1) relax
   (2) warn

3. Michael could have depended on other people, but he made the <u>decision</u> to help himself as much as possible.
   (1) argument
   (2) choice

4. Michael and his family <u>communicated</u> with sign language until he learned to speak.
   (1) talked to each other
   (2) went places together

Writing Skills Mini-Lesson: Using Capital Letters

Sometimes you need to use a **capital letter** at the beginning of a word. Use a capital letter for the following.

1. **The first word of a sentence and the word *I*.**
    There was a fire last year. **My** wife and **I** lost everything.

2. **Days of the week, holidays, and months.**
    Monday, Friday, Labor Day, Thanksgiving Day, January, May

3. **Names of places (cities, states, countries, continents).**
    St. Louis, California, Mexico, Asia

4. **People's names and titles.**
    Mr. David Gelman, the **Hassans, Dr. Julia Estevez**

Practice Copy the paragraph below. Use capital letters following the rules above.

one tuesday last november, there was a terrible fire in springfield. it burned our building and two others to the ground. my wife and i lost everything. our neighbor, evelyn williams, let us stay with her. that week, ms. williams gave us clothes and even made us thanksgiving dinner. she also helped us find a new apartment. in december, my family and i invited her to celebrate kwanzaa in our new home.

_____

_____

_____

_____

_____

_____

▶ Unit 2 Review

Reading Review

This reading is about how one woman coped with a problem caused by being in a wheelchair. Read it and answer the questions that follow.

Where There Is a Will There Is a Way

Isaura Carneiro

Isaura Carneiro lives in Toronto, Canada. She has used a wheelchair since 1979. She learned to read and write English at St. Christopher House Adult Literacy Program. This is a true story written by Isaura. This story has been revised from its original book format.

It was January and a nice sunny day, but cold. I took my electric wheelchair and went to a mall 15 minutes from my apartment. I went to the bank to cash my check and I paid my bills.

On the way home, I passed by McDonald's. I felt like having some food to take home. I was outside by the door for about 5 minutes. Nobody showed up to open the door for me. I was very disappointed because I always think that I can do everything except walk.

Then I had an idea. I said to myself, "I can do it!" I went to the drive-through, which is where people in cars order food. When it buzzed, I ordered what I wanted. When the woman saw me, she started laughing. She said I had a good idea!

I got home with my food and I felt very proud of myself. The fact that I am in a wheelchair doesn't stop me from doing what I want. I just do it in a different way. I am very happy with my life.

Choose the best answer for each question.

1. What was Isaura's problem in her story?
   (1) A woman at McDonald's laughed at her.
   (2) She could not open a door from her wheelchair.

2. Which of these statements describes Isaura?
   (1) She thinks of ways to solve her problems.
   (2) She needs and wants other people to help her.

3. Why was Isaura proud of herself?
   (1) She got back home with her food from McDonald's still warm.
   (2) She had not let her wheelchair keep her from ordering food.

Writing Process

In Unit 2, you wrote three first drafts. Choose the draft that you would like to work with more. You will revise, edit, and make a final copy of this draft.

_____ your note to Rosa (page 46)

_____ your poem about a change you will make (page 53)

_____ your letter to Michael Delani (page 60)

Find the first draft you chose. Then turn to page 128 in this book. Follow steps 3, 4, and 5 in the Writing Process to create a final draft.

As you revise, check your draft for this specific point:

Note: Do you have at least one good piece of advice for Rosa?

Poem: Were you clear about how you are going to change?

Letter: Have you included three good questions?

Unit 3 New Beginnings

We all begin something new sometime in our lives. That is because life is full of change. Change brings the chance for a new beginning.

The move to a new home is a new beginning. So is starting a new job. The birth of a child is a new beginning for both the child and the parents. Life after a divorce is a new beginning. Some new beginnings can be hard. Some can be wonderful.

Before you start Unit 3, think about changes in your life. What new beginnings have you made? What new beginnings are yet to come?

▶ **Be an Active Reader**
As you read the selections in this unit
- Put a question mark (?) by things you do not understand.
- <u>Underline</u> words you do not know. Try to use context clues to figure them out.

Lesson 7

Strategy: Use what you know to understand what you read
Reading: Read the words to a song
Skill: Make inferences
Writing: Write about a song

Before You Read

"Follow the Drinking Gourd" was a song sung by slaves before the Civil War. Its words told how to escape along the Underground Railroad. The Underground Railroad was not a real railroad. It was a secret route. It led from the slave states in the South to the free states and Canada in the North.

The song is really a code. For example, it talks about following a "drinking gourd." The drinking gourd is really the Big Dipper, a group of stars that points to the North Star. The other details in the song refer to landmarks along the way.

The song speaks of an "old man" who will carry people to freedom. We don't know who the "old man" was. A man called Peg Leg Joe taught slaves the song and made markings to help guide them north. Some people think he was the "old man" in the song. Other people think the "old man" referred to Harriet Tubman. Harriet Tubman was a slave who escaped along the Underground Railroad. Then she returned 19 times to help hundreds of other slaves escape. The "old man" could be any of the many people who helped the escaping slaves.

Before you read the song, think of what you already know about the time of slavery. Why do you think slaves would want to escape?

Key Words Read the sentence. Do you know the underlined word?

- A <u>gourd</u> is a plant with a hard shell that can be carved to form a drinking cup.

Use the Strategy
Remember that the words to the song are a code. They give
directions for a way to escape north. Use that knowledge to
help you understand the song.

Follow the Drinking Gourd

HARRIET TUBMAN

Chorus:
> Follow the drinking gourd,
> Follow the drinking gourd.
> For the old man is a-waiting
> For to carry you to freedom
> If you follow the drinking gourd.

When the sun comes back
And the first quail calls,
Follow the drinking gourd.
For the old man is a-waiting
For to carry you to freedom
If you follow the drinking gourd.

(Repeat chorus)

The river bank makes a very good road,
The dead trees show you the way.
Left foot, peg foot, traveling on,
Follow the drinking gourd.

(Repeat chorus)

You know the song gives directions on how to escape to the North. You read about Peg Leg Joe marking the way. What do you think the four lines above mean?

◀ Check-in

The river ends between two hills,
Follow the drinking gourd.
There's another river on the other side,
Follow the drinking gourd.

(Repeat chorus)

When the great big river meets the little river,
Follow the drinking gourd.
For the old man is a-waiting
For to carry you to freedom
If you follow the drinking gourd.

▶ **Final Check-in**

Did you use your knowledge of the Underground Railroad to help you understand the song? Why do you think the directions for using the railroad were hidden in the words to a song?

After You Read

A. Did the Song Make Sense? Reread sections you marked with a question mark (?). Do they make sense now? If not, work through this page and the next with a partner. Then reread the song.

B. Build Your Vocabulary Look at the words you <u>underlined</u>. Can you figure them out now? If not, find out what they are. Add them to your word bank.

C. Answer These Questions

1. Think of what you know about the Underground Railroad. What does the song line "The river bank makes a very good road" probably mean?

    (1) A railroad will be built along the river.

    (2) Slaves should walk along the river.

2. What is the drinking gourd leading slaves to?

    (1) freedom

    (2) an old man

3. Why do you think the song keeps repeating "Follow the drinking gourd"?

    (1) to hide the real meaning of the song

    (2) to stress that the slaves should keep following the North Star

4. Why was the song in code?

    (1) so the slaves could memorize it easily

    (2) so the escape route could be kept secret

▶ **Talk About It**

Discuss the question below with a partner or small group. If you like, write a response.

What new beginning does the song refer to?

Think About It: Make Inferences

In Lesson 6, you saw that clues in written material can help you **infer,** or figure out, information that is not actually stated. For example:

• Did the slaves travel during the day or at night?

You can infer the answer to this question. Use clues in the song, as well as what you already know.

Use clues: The song says to follow the "drinking gourd." The "drinking gourd" is the Big Dipper, a group of stars. Since stars are seen only at night, you can infer that the slaves traveled at night.

Use what you already know: It made sense for escaping slaves to travel at night because the darkness would help hide them.

Practice Choose the best answer for each question.

1. Think of what you read about Peg Leg Joe. What does the song line "Left foot, peg foot, traveling on" mean?
   (1) Peg Leg Joe left prints to follow with his good leg and his peg leg.
   (2) Peg Leg Joe had lost his left foot and wore a peg foot in its place.

2. What should the slaves do when the river ends between two hills?
   (1) Wait for an old man to take them to freedom.
   (2) Follow the river that begins on the other side.

3. Why did the slaves call the Big Dipper the "drinking gourd"?
   (1) They used gourds for dippers.
   (2) It looked like a pitcher.

Read "Follow the Drinking Gourd" aloud. Do you understand it better now? Read it with a friend, if you like.

Write About It: Write About a Song

In "Follow the Drinking Gourd," you read a song that was once sung by slaves. Now write down your thoughts about the song.

A. Prewrite Take time to think about "Follow the Drinking Gourd." Here are some questions you might answer:
- What did you like about the song?
- Why was it a good idea to hide the escape directions in a song?
- How would the slaves have felt as they "followed the drinking gourd"?
- What would you like to know more about?

B. Write Write down your thoughts about the song. Use the sentence starters below if you like.

The song "Follow the Drinking Gourd" made me think. I liked

_____

_____

It was a good idea to hide directions for escaping in a song because

_____

_____

The slaves who escaped must have felt _____

_____

I would like to know more about _____

_____

▶ **Hold on to this work.** You may use it again at the end of this unit.

Lesson 8

LEARNING GOALS

Strategy: Imagine what you read
Reading: Read a journal
Skill: Understand the main idea and details
Writing: Write a journal entry
Word Work: Compound words

Before You Read

"Al's Journal" tells about a man whose wife has left him. The man is writing in his journal. In a journal, people write down their thoughts and feelings. Journals are usually private pieces of writing.

Before you read "Al's Journal," think about when one person leaves another. Perhaps something like this has happened to you or someone you know.

A. Imagine someone you love has gone away and left you. What are some of the feelings you might have?

_____

_____

B. In "Al's Journal," do you think you will read the wife's side of the story? Why or why not?

_____

_____

Key Words Read each sentence. Do you know the underlined words?
- My <u>marriage</u> to my wife Sue was ending in <u>divorce</u>.
- The <u>support group</u> helps me share my feelings with others.

Use the Strategy

To help you understand "Al's Journal," imagine you can see and hear the things that are happening. Imagine what it must be like to be Al. Ask yourself, "How would I feel? What would I do?"

Al's Journal

June 1

This has been the worst day of my life. This afternoon, Sue left me. She said good-bye and loaded the suitcases in the car. I watched as she and the girls drove out of the driveway.

Later, I walked through the house. It was so empty. I found Amy's stuffed bear. How will Amy sleep without her bear?

I should have seen this coming. Sue and I have not been happy for a while. We fight too much. Sue is always crying. I thought things would get better. They only got worse.

June 6

Sue is going to file for divorce. She feels there is no hope for us. She says we should both get on with our lives.

I asked Sue if there was another man. She said no. She says she is very unhappy. She doesn't want to be with me or anyone else right now. I see now that our marriage had been in trouble for a long time.

Check-in ▶ Could you see Sue and the children leaving? Did you picture Al walking through the empty house? Can you imagine how he feels?

June 9

I am worried about the girls. Amy is only 5 years old. Jane is just 7. They are not handling the divorce well. They do not understand. Jane thinks I am angry with her. I keep telling her that her mom and I both love her. I want her to know it's not her fault. But she is still upset.

Amy is having a hard time too. Last night on the phone, she asked, "When are we coming home, Daddy?" I didn't know what to say.

June 20

I joined a support group today. The group is for men going through a divorce. It meets Monday evenings in the same office building I work in. Joe at work told me about it. I didn't want to join. But I didn't know what else to do. I have been feeling lost.

The first meeting was strange. I felt out of place. I did not want to talk about my life in front of six men I don't even know.

June 27

Today I went to the second meeting of my support group. I felt better. The men in the group really understand. They gave me good advice. They even had some ideas about how I can help the girls.

I still daydream about the way things were. I wish I could go back and do things differently. But I can't. Maybe with the group's help, I can move on with my life.

▶ **Final Check-in**

Did you try to see the events and hear people speak as you read? Could you imagine Al's worry about his children? How did he look and feel when he went to the support group?

After You Read

A. Did the Journal Make Sense? Reread sections you marked with a question mark (?). Do they make sense now? If not, discuss them with a partner or your instructor.

B. Build Your Vocabulary Look at the words you <u>underlined</u>. Can you figure them out now? If not, find out what they are. Add them to your word bank.

C. Answer These Questions

1. Choose how you imagined Al felt on June 1.
   (1) hopeful
   (2) rested
   (3) shocked

2. Choose how Al had changed by June 27.
   (1) He was more hopeful about his new life.
   (2) He was going to try to win his wife back.
   (3) He did not feel good about the people in his support group.

3. List two or three things you think Al discussed in his support group meetings.

_____

_____

_____

▶ **Talk About It**

Discuss the questions below with a partner or small group.
If you like, write a response.

Do you think writing in a journal helped Al? Why or why not?
What advice would you give to Al?

Think About It: Understand the Main Idea and Details

In Lesson 2 you saw that the **main idea** is the most important point in a piece of writing. **Details** are pieces of information that help support or explain the main idea. Sometimes the main idea is stated. Sometimes you have to put it in your own words.

For example, read the June 6 entry in Al's journal.

> ▶ Sue is going to file for divorce. She feels there is no hope for us. She says we should both get on with our lives.
>
> I asked Sue if there was another man. She said no. She says she is very unhappy. She doesn't want to be with me or anyone else right now. I see now that our marriage had been in trouble for a long time.

Choose the main idea of Al's journal entry on June 6:
  (1) Al does not trust his wife.
  (2) Al and Sue's marriage is ending.
  (3) Sue says there is not another man.

The main idea is (2) Al and Sue's marriage is ending. Most of the sentences tell about a marriage that is ending. They describe an unhappy wife.

Go back to the June 6 entry. Underline three details that support the idea of a marriage that is ending.

You could have underlined any three of these details:
  • Sue is going to file for divorce.
  • She feels there is no hope for us.
  • She says we should both get on with our lives.
  • She says she is very unhappy.
  • She doesn't want to be with me or anyone else right now.
  • Our marriage had been in trouble for a long time.

Practice

A. Read this June 9 entry from Al's journal again.

> ▶ I am worried about the girls. Amy is only 5 years old. Jane is just 7. They are not handling the divorce well. They do not understand. Jane thinks I am angry with her. I keep telling her that her mom and I both love her. I want her to know it's not her fault. But she is still upset.
>
> Amy is having a hard time too. Last night on the phone, she asked, "When are we coming home, Daddy?" I didn't know what to say.

1. What is the main idea of the journal entry?
   (1) Children think they are to blame for a divorce.
   (2) Al's children are 5 and 7.
   (3) Al's children are not handling the divorce well.

2. Underline three details in the entry that support the main idea.

B. Here is the main idea of a news story:
Marriages fail for many reasons.

Read the details in the box below. Then on the lines, write the three details that fit the main idea.

Some couples marry too young.	Some couples do not talk enough.
Not all couples are unhappy.	Couples often share interests.
Sometimes couples grow apart.	Not all people get married.

1. Detail: _____

2. Detail: _____

3. Detail: _____

Write About It: Write a Journal Entry

In this lesson, you read the journal of a man whose wife had left him.
Every few days, he wrote about his thoughts and feelings in his journal.

Now write a journal entry yourself. Think about a time when you had to
face something very hard. What was it? How did you feel? How did it turn
out? How do you feel about the problem today? You may want to jot some
notes down.

_____

_____

_____

Write Write a journal entry about this time in your life.

Date: _____

_____

_____

_____

_____

_____

_____

_____

_____

▶ **Hold on to this work.** You may decide that you want to share it with others.

Word Work: Compound Words

A **compound word** is a word made up of two smaller words. For example, *bedroom* is made up of *bed* and *room*. When you are reading and you come to a long word you don't recognize, look for smaller words in it that you do know. Sometimes you will be able to figure out the word that way.

A. There are several compound words in Al's journal. Read the three below.

afternoon   suitcases   driveway

1. Draw a line between the two smaller words in each compound word. Then write the two words that make up the compound word. The first one is started for you.

   a. after|noon   ___after___   _____

   b. suitcases   _____   _____

   c. driveway   _____   _____

2. Look through "Al's Journal." Find two more compound words. Write them below. Next, draw a line between the two smaller words in each compound word. Then write the two words that make up the compound word.

Compound Word	**First Word**	**Second Word**
a. _____	_____	_____
b. _____	_____	_____

B. Underline the word in each row that is not a compound word. Draw a line between the two parts of each compound word. The first row is started for you.

1. <u>unhappy</u>   week|end   sunscreen   paycheck

2. backyard   bathtub   newsstand   worried

3. doorway   meeting   haircut   peacemaker

Lesson 9

LEARNING GOALS

Strategy: Retell
Reading: Read a student's autobiography
Skill: Make inferences
Writing: Conduct and write an interview
Word Work: Prefixes and roots

Before You Read

"A New World" is an autobiography by Mamie Chow. An autobiography is the true story of the author's own life. Mamie came from China to the United States. She began a new life in a new country. Mamie is now an adult student. Here is her story.

Before you read "A New World," think about a person who has moved to a new country. Perhaps you are such a person, or perhaps you know someone who is.

A. What kind of problem may this person have with each of these things?

language _____

job _____

getting around _____

friends _____

B. List other topics you might read about or you hope to read about in "A New World."

_____

Key Words Read each sentence. Do you know the underlined words?
- My parents <u>arranged</u> for me to leave China.
- We ran a <u>laundry</u> <u>business</u> that made money.

A New World

Mamie Chow

When I first came to the United States, life was strange. Everything was new—the country, the language, the customs. I had to learn everything all over again.

I left China in 1948. My parents arranged it. They wanted what was best for me. China was in ruins after the war. There was no work. There wasn't even enough food for everyone.

In the old days, young girls in China had their marriages arranged by their parents. I had never said a word to my parents about men. My mother had me dress up for a photograph. I didn't know why she wanted the picture. I learned later that she had sent it to a Chinese man living in New York.

One morning my mother dressed me up to go to town. We walked back and forth in front of a store. The man from New York had come to China to see me. He and his friends were inside the store watching me. I guess he liked me. Two weeks later we got married.

Check-in ► Think about what you have just read. What things have you learned about Mamie Chow's life?

About six months later, we left China. I was pregnant. The boat took two weeks to get to San Francisco, California. Then we took a plane to Newark, New Jersey. All the travel made me dizzy but I was happy to come to New York City. I could have a job and make a living for my family.

My only problem was that I didn't speak English—not even a word. At first, I would only go out with my husband.

Still, there was so much to see. Some buildings were tall. Some buildings were low. Some buildings were very old. The subways were old and creaky and had cane seats. But they were safe and only cost a nickel.

In 1954, my husband and I bought a laundry from people we knew. The price was $2,500. We borrowed all of the money. We were tricked. After we ran the business a few months, someone came to tell us that the city was going to tear down the building. We were shocked. We were lucky to find a new store. That one turned out OK.

What has happened to Mamie Chow since she came to the United States?

◀ **Check-in**

I had three children. It was hard for us but the whole family helped make our business a success.

When my older daughter got off school, she would take care of her baby brother. She would play with him, bathe him, and cook the family dinner. Later she would do her homework.

My husband and I worked late every day. I stood all day to do the laundry. I got tired and my feet hurt. Sometimes we got home at 12:30 A.M. That was my life for 30 years.

Now I'm retired and can do what I like. After so many years in this new country, I am finally working on my language skills. I am proud of how far I have come.

▶ **Final Check-in**

Can you remember enough of Mamie Chow's story to tell it to someone else? Tell her story in your own words to a partner.

After You Read

A. Did the Story Make Sense? Reread sections you marked with a
question mark (?). Do they make sense now? If not, discuss them
with a partner or your instructor.

B. Build Your Vocabulary Look at the words you <u>underlined</u>. Can you
figure them out now? If not, find out what they are. Add them to your
word bank.

C. Answer These Questions

1. Write the three most important things you would tell somebody
   about Mamie Chow's life.

   _____

   _____

   _____

2. Check each word below that you think describes Mamie Chow.

   _____ funny   _____ gloomy   _____ hard-working

   _____ proud   _____ forgetful   _____ down-to-earth

3. Do you think Mamie Chow will succeed at improving her language
   skills? Finish the sentence. Tell why or why not.

   I think Mamie Chow _____

   _____

   ▶ **Talk About It**

   Discuss the questions below with a partner or small group.
   If you like, write a response.

   Mamie Chow made a successful new beginning. Do you think
   her life is like the lives of many other people who have made
   new beginnings in this country? Why or why not?

Think About It: Make Inferences

You have seen that sometimes you can figure out facts and ideas that are not directly stated. Clues in the reading can help you to **make inferences.**

Read this part of Mamie Chow's story again. Try to infer the kind of daughter Mamie was.

▶ In the old days, young girls in China had their marriages arranged by their parents. I had never said a word to my parents about men. My mother had me dress up for a photograph. I didn't know why she wanted the picture. I learned later that she had sent it to a Chinese man living in New York.

Yes	No	You can infer that:
_____	_____	Mamie was a quiet daughter who kept her feelings to herself.
_____	_____	Mamie did not like her mother.
_____	_____	Mamie obeyed her parents.
_____	_____	Mamie did not argue with her parents.

These clues show that Mamie kept her feelings to herself and obeyed her parents. She did not argue with them.
- I had never said a word to my parents about men.
- My mother had me dress up for a photograph.
- I didn't know why she wanted the picture.

But there are no clues that Mamie did not like her mother. You would not have a good reason to infer that.

Practice

Read these parts from Mamie Chow's story again. Check **Yes** for each idea
that you can infer from clues in the story. Check **No** for ideas that cannot
be inferred.

▶ About six months later, we left China. I was pregnant. The boat took
two weeks to get to San Francisco, California. Then we took a plane
to Newark, New Jersey. All the travel made me dizzy but I was happy
to come to New York City. I could have a job and make a living for
my family.

My only problem was that I didn't speak English—not even a word.
At first, I would only go out with my husband.

Yes   **No**

_____   _____

_____   _____

_____   _____

You can infer that:
1. Mamie accepted marriage and family duty.
2. Mamie thought of herself before others.
3. Mamie's husband spoke English.

▶ I had three children. It was hard for us but the whole family helped make
our business a success.

When my older daughter got off school, she would take care of her baby
brother. She would play with him, bathe him, and cook the family
dinner. Later she would do her homework.

My husband and I worked late every day. I stood all day to do the
laundry. I got tired and my feet hurt. Sometimes we got home at
12:30 A.M. That was my life for 30 years.

Yes   **No**

_____   _____

_____   _____

_____   _____

You can infer that:
4. Mamie didn't care about her children.
5. The children were often without their mother.
6. Mamie is proud of her older daughter.

Write About It: Conduct and Write an Interview

In "A New World," you read about a woman who made a new beginning in life. Think of a new beginning you have made. Choose one of these beginnings, or think of one of your own.

getting married   moving   getting divorced

returning to school   having a child   getting a new job

Work with a partner. Take turns interviewing each other about your new beginnings.

A. Prewrite Think about the question words *who, what, when, where,* and *why.* Write three questions you will ask your partner about his or her new beginning.

_____

_____

_____

Use the questions you wrote to interview your partner. Take notes on the answers on a separate paper.

B. Write Write about your partner's answers here.

_____

_____

_____

_____

_____

_____

▶ **Hold on to this work.** You may use it again at the end of this unit.

Word Work: Prefixes and Roots

A **root** is the word part that carries the basic meaning. A **prefix** is a word part that is added to the beginning of a root. The prefix plus the root make a new word with a different meaning. For example, when the prefix *un-* is added to the root *able*, we have the new word *unable*, meaning *not able*.

When you come to a word you don't recognize, see if it has a prefix and root. Cover the prefix and read the root first. Then add the prefix to read the whole word.

If you add the meaning of the prefix to the meaning of the root word, you can figure out what the new word means. Look at the examples below.

Prefix	Meaning	Example	New Meaning
un-	not	unhappy	not happy
re-	again	reheat	heat again
anti-	against	antislavery	against slavery

A. Add the prefix to each root below. Write the new word.

1. un + usual _____

2. anti + drug _____

3. re + play _____

4. un + kind _____

5. re + build _____

6. un + sure _____

7. anti + freeze _____

8. re + produce _____

B. Draw a line between the prefix and root in each word below. Read the words.

1. reread

2. antisocial

3. unpleasant

4. refuel

5. antiseptic

6. unfamiliar

7. unnecessary

8. rearrange

▶ Writing Skills Mini-Lesson: Writing Sentences

To write a correct, complete sentence, follow these rules.

1. **Write a complete thought.**

   Not Complete: To prepare for a career.
   Complete: I am taking classes to prepare for a career.

2. **Include a subject (telling who or what the sentence is about) and a verb (telling what the subject does or is).**

          S   V
   This **school offers** computer courses.

   S V
   I am a student in this school.

   S   V
   I have taken many classes here.

          S   V
   The **instructor** in room 104 **teaches** well.

3. **Start with a capital letter and end with a period (.), question mark (?), or exclamation point (!).**

   It is ten o'clock. Where were you? You missed the exam!

Practice On your own paper, rewrite the following as correct, complete sentences.

1. improve my reading and writing skills

2. recently, I back to school

3. a good career

4. what are going to study

5. I am interested in

Unit 3 Review

Reading Review

This reading is about a new beginning. Read it and then answer the questions.

The Empty Nest

Jim and Nancy Zack's daughter, Ann, had just started her first year of college. She was going to school in another state. During the first few weeks, Ann called home almost every day. She was lonely and scared. "New beginnings can be very hard," Nancy would tell her daughter. "Give yourself time to get used to the changes in your life."

Nancy knew how Ann was feeling. She was having trouble getting used to the change in her life too. Ann was the last of their children to leave home. Sometimes Nancy found herself setting a plate for Ann at the dinner table. Then tears would begin to sting her eyes.

Deep down, Nancy knew they would all get used to this change. She also knew this was a special time for her and Jim. Their "nest" was now empty. Their children were gone. They, too, were going through a new beginning. "I'll just give myself time to get used to the changes in my life," Nancy reminded herself with a smile.

Choose the best answer for each question.

1. Which title would be best for this story?
   (1) New Beginnings for the Zack Family
   (2) The Empty Nest Problem
   (3) Ann's First Year at School

2. Why would Nancy sometimes cry when setting a plate for Ann?
   (1) She knew she would never see Ann again.
   (2) She felt she was getting old and forgetting a lot.
   (3) She realized Ann was gone and missed her.

3. What kind of mother do you think Nancy is?

    (1) in control and demanding

    (2) cold and not caring

    (3) caring and understanding

Writing Process

In Unit 3, you wrote three things. Choose the piece that you would like to work with more. You will revise, edit, and make a final copy of this draft.

    _____ your thoughts about the song (page 71)

    _____ your journal entry about something hard that you had to face (page 78)

    _____ your interview about your partner's new beginning (page 86)

Find the first draft you chose. Then turn to page 128 in this book. Follow steps 3, 4, and 5 in the Writing Process to create a final draft.

As you revise, check your draft for this specific point:

Thoughts about the song: Did you make your thoughts about the song clear?

Journal entry: Did you explain how you felt before and how you feel now?

Interview: Did you include the answers to all your questions?

Unit 4   Celebrate Differences

America is home to many cultures. America is special because of this. Its people are of different races. They believe in different religions. Its people have different cultural backgrounds. We can celebrate these differences. They help make America a rich and interesting place to live.

Before you start Unit 4, think about your cultural background. How does your culture help make you who you are? Do you have special holidays and other customs that are part of your culture? Do your friends belong to different cultures? If so, how do their customs differ from yours? How are they the same?

▶ **Be an Active Reader**

As you read the selections in this unit
- Put a question mark (?) by things you do not understand.
- <u>Underline</u> words you do not know. Try to use context clues to figure them out.

Lesson 10

Before You Read

"Neighborly Celebrations" is a story about three different celebrations that take place in December. All three celebrations are rich in family traditions. Christmas is a holiday celebrated on December 25. Christians celebrate the birth of Jesus Christ. During the Christmas season, people decorate their homes with trees and lights, and families gather to eat and exchange gifts.

Many African Americans also celebrate Kwanzaa [KWAHN zah], a celebration of cultural values. It begins on December 26 and lasts for seven days. Kwanzaa combines African customs and African American ideals and goals. During Kwanzaa, families gather each evening and light one candle in the *kinara*. They give gifts and discuss important ideas for the community. On December 31, they have a feast called the *karamu*.

Jewish families celebrate Hanukkah [HAHN uh kuh] in December. It is the Feast of Lights and lasts for eight days. Hanukkah celebrates an event in Jewish history. Each night a candle is lighted in the *menorah*. People retell the ancient stories, eat traditional foods, and give gifts.

Before you read "Neighborly Celebrations," write the name of a holiday you celebrate. List two or three things you do to celebrate it.

_____

_____

Use the Strategy

This story tells how people of different cultures celebrate their holidays. To help you understand the story, think of holidays you celebrate. Compare your celebration with the way the people in the story celebrate.

Neighborly Celebrations

Paul was walking home from a fast-food place. He was sad. It was December. Here he was, all alone, eating fast-food chicken. Paul had just moved to this city. He couldn't go home for Christmas. And he hadn't made any new friends to spend the holiday with.

As Paul unlocked his apartment door, the door across the hall opened. Out stepped a young couple. Paul paused. Then he decided to say something.

Check-in ▶ How does Paul's experience compare with your own? Have you ever been away from home during a traditional family holiday?

"That's a beautiful candle holder in your window," Paul said. He had seen their lighted candles from the street below. "It has a special meaning, doesn't it?"

The man looked up. "Yes," he said. "It's called a menorah. It's for our Jewish holiday of Hanukkah."

"Oh," Paul said. "I celebrate Christmas myself. Except for this year. I just moved here. I don't have anyone to spend Christmas Day with next week."

"We have the same problem," the woman said. "We couldn't fly home for Hanukkah. I'll miss my father's cooking. He makes the best potato pancakes."

"I know what you mean," laughed Paul. "My mom makes a great plum pudding. By the way, I'm Paul Black."

"We're Barry and Brenda Kahn," the man said.

Just then a woman coming along stopped. "Hi. I'm Wanda Mays. I live down the hall. I hope you don't mind, but I heard you talking. It sounds like we all have the same problem. Only one of my children can come for the holidays this year."

Paul invited them all into his apartment. They each began to talk about holiday memories. Paul spoke of Christmas Eve. He told how his family sang carols. "Even as an adult, I can hardly wait for Christmas morning to open presents."

"During the eight days of Hanukkah, we used to meet at my parents' house," Brenda told them. "We would light another candle each evening until all eight were lit."

"As kids, we got coins and other gifts, too," Barry added.

Wanda spoke of the holiday she and her daughter would celebrate soon. "Kwanzaa lasts for seven days. We also light candles each night, and we discuss the seven principles of Kwanzaa. We give each other gifts we have made. On the last day, we have a feast. But it won't seem the same this year."

How do the experiences of Paul, Brenda, Barry, and Wanda compare with your own?

◀ **Check-in**

"I have an idea!" said Brenda. "Let's celebrate our own special holiday together! You can come to our place this Sunday. We will each make special food that we usually have with our families. And we'll each share a special custom from our holiday. What do you think?"

Wanda jumped up. "That's a great idea!"

Paul smiled. "I'm better at reheating fast food than making plum pudding. But I can buy one at the bakery. Let's do it!"

▶ **Final Check-in**

Did your own holiday experiences help you understand the story? How do your experiences compare with those of the characters in the story?

After You Read

A. Did the Story Make Sense? Reread sections you marked with a question mark (?). Do they make sense now? If not, discuss them with a partner or your instructor.

B. Build Your Vocabulary Look at the words you <u>underlined</u>. Can you figure them out now? If not, find out what they are. Add them to your word bank.

C. Answer These Questions

1. Check each way your holiday celebrations are like the celebrations of one or more of the characters.

_____ family gatherings   _____ make gifts   _____ sing songs

_____ tell stories   _____ light candles   _____ give gifts

_____ special food   _____ religious services

2. What was Paul's problem in the story?

_____

3. What does Paul do that helps solve his problem?

_____

_____

4. What does Brenda do to help solve the problem?

_____

_____

 Talk About It

Discuss the questions below with a partner or small group.
If you like, write a response.

What was different about the characters' holiday celebrations?
How were the celebrations alike?

Think About It: Understand Plot and Character

In Lesson 1 you learned that the **plot** of a story is what happens in the story. The plot follows a plan that has three important parts. They can be pictured like this:

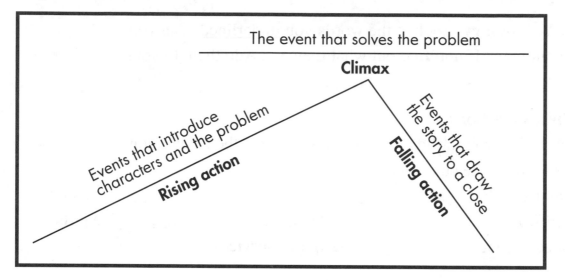

In Lesson 4 you learned that you may find out one or more of these things about the **characters,** or people in a story:

- looks
- backgrounds
- what they think
- the kind of people they are
- how they deal with life

The author may tell you about these things directly. Or you may infer them from what a character does and says.

Practice Answer these questions about the plot and characters of "Neighborly Celebrations."

1. What is the main problem in the story?
    (1) The characters won't be with their families for the holidays.
    (2) Paul does not know Brenda and Barry Kahn.
    (3) The neighbors don't get along with each other.

2. What event marks the climax of the story?
    (1) Paul and the Kahns talk about holidays.
    (2) Wanda steps into the group.
    (3) Brenda says, "Let's celebrate our own special holiday together!"

3. What happens after the climax?

   (1) Brenda tells of her father's cooking.

   (2) They all agree to celebrate together.

   (3) Paul and his neighbors talk about their holidays.

4. Write your answers to questions 1–3 on the correct lines below.

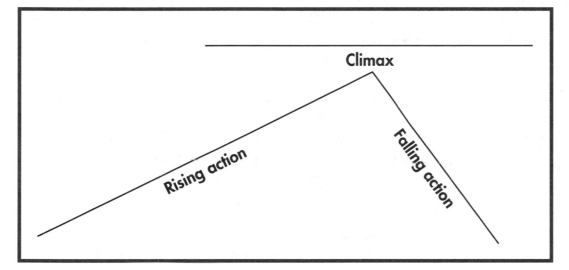

5. Name the characters in "Neighborly Celebrations." Write the main character first.

   _____   _____

   _____   _____

6. Complete this character web of Paul. Write three words or phrases that describe him.

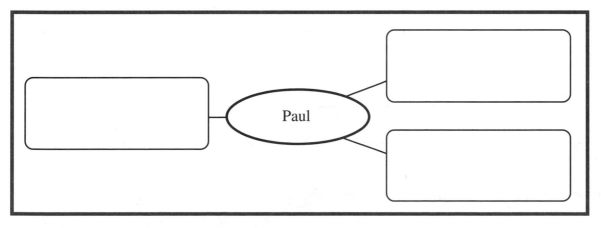

7. Retell the story "Neighborly Celebrations" to a partner. Use your plot diagram and character web to help you.

Write About It: Write a Description

In "Neighborly Celebrations," characters explained how they celebrated holidays. Now write a description about a holiday you celebrate.

A. Prewrite Think about your favorite holiday. Complete this idea map about the holiday.

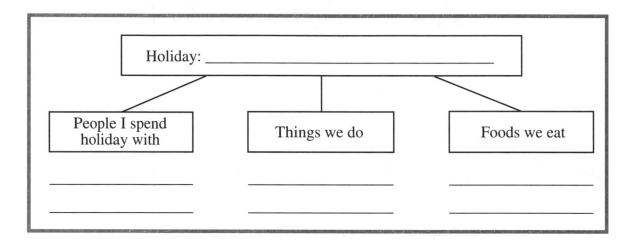

B. Write Use your idea map to describe your favorite holiday.

My favorite holiday is _____

I spend the day with _____

We celebrate by _____

_____

_____

For our holiday meal, we have _____

_____

_____

▶ **Hold on to this work.** You may use it again at the end of this unit.

Word Work: Suffixes -ful, -less, -able, -or

A **suffix** is a word part that is added to the end of a root. The suffix and the root word form a new word. For example, when the suffix -ful is added to the root word care, we have the new word careful.

When you are reading and come to a word you don't recognize, see if it has a root word and an ending. If so, cover the ending and read the root first. Then add the ending to read the whole word.

Suffixes can change the meaning of the root. Look at the examples in this chart.

Suffix	Meaning	Example	New Meaning
-ful	full of	hopeful	full of hope
-less	without	hopeless	without hope
-able	capable	allowable	to be allowed
-or	person who	operator	person who operates

A. Add the suffix to each word below. Write the new word. You may have to drop a final silent e before adding a suffix that begins with a vowel.

1. create + or _____

2. help + less _____

3. depend + able _____

4. success + ful _____

5. use + ful _____

6. adore + able _____

7. care + less _____

8. counsel + or _____

B. Draw a line between the suffix and root word in each word below.

1. sorrowful   3. agreeable   5. profitable   7. useless

2. breathless   4. spectator   6. thoughtful   8. actor

Lesson 11

LEARNING GOALS

Strategy: Use what you know to understand what you read
Reading: Read a biography
Skill: Make inferences
Writing: Write your autobiography
Word Work: The suffix -ion

Before You Read

"Celebrate an American Life" is a biography of Senator Daniel Inouye [IN oo ay], a Japanese American. Remember that a biography is a true story about a real person. It contains facts about the person's life.

A. Before you read "Celebrate an American Life," think about the kind of information you read in a biography. Write two or three facts you expect to learn from a biography. One fact is already written.

<u>where the person was born</u>   _____

_____   _____

B. Now check each topic you might read about in the biography of a Japanese American.

_____ details about his culture   _____ when his family came to live in America

_____ how he grew up   _____ places to visit in Japan

Key Words Read each sentence. Do you know the underlined words?

- <u>Hawaii</u> is made up of many <u>islands</u> in the <u>Pacific Ocean</u>.
- If you work hard, you have the <u>opportunity</u> to succeed.
- He was elected <u>senator</u> from his home state.

Celebrate an American Life

Hawaii is an island chain in the Pacific Ocean. It is very beautiful. Its people come from many different places. They are of many cultures and religions. Here, on September 7, 1924, Daniel Inouye was born. His parents were both from Japan.

DANIEL INOUYE

Young Daniel grew up in both the Japanese and American cultures. He learned to speak Japanese before he learned English. Like other children, Daniel went to public school. He also went to a Japanese school for two hours every day. There he studied Japanese history and customs. He learned to read and write Japanese. But Daniel knew that his parents also shared American beliefs. They taught their children that opportunity waited for "those who had the heart and strength."

Check-in ► Did the first part of the biography tell you what you thought it would? What do you think you will learn next about Daniel Inouye?

While Daniel was growing up in Hawaii, events were happening in the rest of the world that would have a great impact on his life. In 1937, Japan invaded China. In 1939, war broke out in Europe.

In December 1941, Daniel was a senior in high school. He dreamed of becoming a doctor. However, on December 7, something happened that would later ruin his dream. About 8 A.M. that day, Japanese planes bombed U.S. ships in Hawaii's Pearl Harbor. Thousands of U.S. troops died in the attack. It was the start of World War II for Americans.

Many Japanese Americans were ashamed of what Japan had done. They were loyal to the U.S. They wanted to join the army. Inouye was one of them. But tension in the country ran high. Many other Americans distrusted all Japanese. Japanese Americans were not allowed in the armed forces. Inouye went to college instead. In time, the ban on Japanese Americans in the armed forces ended. Then Inouye left school and joined the army. After training, he was sent to Italy to fight.

What information have you read about Daniel Inouye so far? What part of his life do you think you will read about next?

◀ Check-in

In April 1945, Inouye led his men into a fierce battle. He was hit by gunfire many times. His right arm was shattered. But Inouye kept fighting. After the battle, Inouye's arm could not be saved. His dream of becoming a doctor would never come true.

After the war, Inouye went to law school. There he met his future wife. She was one of the teachers. "I proposed on our second date," he recalled.

Inouye became a lawyer. He also helped lead the drive to make Hawaii the 50th state. In 1959, at the age of 34, Inouye was voted Hawaii's first U.S. senator. He also became the first Japanese American to serve in Congress. He would serve as a senator for more than 35 years.

Senator Inouye was once asked what he would tell today's students. He recalled what his father told him the day he left for the army: "This country has been good to us. We owe much to this country. And now . . . it is you who must try to return the goodness of this country." Daniel Inouye followed his father's advice—again and again.

▶ **Final Check-in**
Did you find the kind of information you expected to find in the biography of Daniel Inouye?

After You Read

A. Did the Biography Make Sense? Reread sections you marked with
a question mark(?). Do they make sense now? If not, discuss them
with a partner or your instructor.

B. Build Your Vocabulary Look at the words you <u>underlined</u>. Can you
figure them out now? If not, find out what they are. Add them to your
word bank.

C. Answer These Questions

1. Check each type of information you read about in Senator Inouye's
   biography.

   _____ where he was born   _____ what his childhood was like

   _____ when he was born   _____ how many children he has

   _____ what he likes to do   _____ what he does for a living

2. Choose the best description of Senator Inouye's life.

   (1) He is a Japanese American who has served his country in many ways.

   (2) He was born to Japanese parents and learned Japanese before English.

   (3) He lost the use of his arm in World War II.

3. Write two words or phrases that describe Senator Inouye.

   _____

   _____

 Talk About It

Discuss the questions below with a partner or small group.
If you like, write a response.

Discrimination is treating a whole group of people differently
because of their race, culture, religion, or sex. When did
Daniel Inouye face discrimination? Was this discrimination right?
Why or why not?

Think About It: Make Inferences

You know that clues in writing can help you **infer,** or figure out, information. In "Celebrate an American Life," you read how one Japanese American served his country. Now look at this cartoon. What can you infer about the many different cultures in America?

Can you infer from the cartoon that customs from many different cultures have enriched the American way of life? _____

The man speaking lists things we eat and use in America. We may think of these things as being American. However, many of them come from other cultures. So you can infer that other cultures have enriched American culture.

Practice Read each selection. Then check whether or not you can infer each idea.

▶ Young Daniel grew up in both the Japanese and American cultures. He learned to speak Japanese before he learned English. Like other children, Daniel went to public school. He also went to a Japanese school for two hours every day. There he studied Japanese history and customs. He learned to read and write Japanese. But Daniel knew that his parents also shared American beliefs. They taught their children that opportunity waited for "those who had the heart and strength."

Yes	No	**You can infer that:**
_____	_____	1. Daniel's parents thought education and the family's culture were important.
_____	_____	2. His parents thought Japanese culture was better than American culture.

▶ Inouye became a lawyer. He also helped lead the drive to make Hawaii the 50th state. In 1959, at the age of 34, Inouye was voted Hawaii's first U.S. senator. He also became the first Japanese American to serve in Congress. He would serve as a senator for more than 35 years.

Yes	No	**You can infer that:**
_____	_____	3. Hawaii became a state around 1959.
_____	_____	4. Daniel Inouye was re-elected senator.

▶ **Talk About It**

Discuss the question below with a partner or small group.
If you like, write a response.

Think about your own cultural group. What kinds of things has it given to the American way of life?

Write About It: Write Your Autobiography

In "Celebrate an American Life," you read a biography about Senator Daniel Inouye. When someone writes about his or her own life, it is called an **autobiography.** Now write a short autobiography about yourself and your cultural background.

A. Prewrite Think about the facts you would include in your autobiography. Some facts are suggested below.

When were you born? _____

Where were you born? _____

Where did you grow up? _____

What is your family's cultural background? _____

What is a favorite cultural custom? _____

B. Write Now write a short autobiography. Use your answers above and these sentence starters to help you. Add other information if you like.

I was born on _____

in _____ I grew up in _____

_____

My family came from _____

_____

I have always enjoyed our custom of _____

_____

_____

▶ **Hold on to this work.** You may use it again at the end of this unit.

Word Work: The Suffix -ion

In Lesson 10, you learned that a suffix is a word part added to the end of a root. The new word has a different meaning and is used in a different way from the root. For example:

- The **great** man was **greatly** admired.

Many words end with the suffix -ion. The suffix -ion indicates an act or process, a result, or a state or condition. Words with the suffix -ion usually end with the sound *shun*.

- elect + ion = election
- tense + ion = tension

(Note that the final silent *e* is dropped when -ion is added.)

The suffix -ion usually changes the way a word is used in a sentence.

- Hawaii will **elect** a senator during this **election.**
- People were so **tense** you could feel the **tension.**

A. Add -ion to each word below. Write the new word. You may have to drop a final *e*. Then read the words.

1. direct _____   4. react _____

2. discuss _____   5. locate _____ _____

3. confuse _____   6. inspect _____

B. Split each of these words into a root and a suffix. You may have to add -e to the root word.

1. adoption   = _____ + _____

2. celebration = _____ + _____

3. completion = _____ + _____

C. On another paper, write three more words that end in -ion. Break each into a root and a suffix.

Lesson 12

LEARNING GOALS

Strategy: Use what you know to understand what you read
Reading: Read two poems
Skill: Identify rhyme, rhythm, and repetition
Writing: Write a poem

Before You Read

In this lesson, you will read two poems: "Manhattan" and "You've Got to Be Carefully Taught." Both poems deal with people of different cultures and races.

The poem "Manhattan" is about a part of New York City. For many years, people coming from other countries to the U.S. have landed in New York. In Manhattan, you can see people from just about every country on earth.

The poem "You've Got to Be Carefully Taught" is a song from the musical play *South Pacific*. It is sung by an American soldier. He loves a young woman. But he won't marry her because she is of a different race. An American nurse says that people are "born" with such prejudice against other races. Then the soldier realizes that both he and the nurse are wrong. He says, "It's not born in you! It happens *after* you're born." And he sings "You've Got to Be Carefully Taught."

Before you read the two poems, think of how people act toward others of different races. Write one example you have seen of people acting with respect. Write one example of people acting from prejudice.

Respect

Prejudice

_____   _____

Key Words Read these sentences. Do you know the underlined words?
- New York is a <u>wondrous</u> city with many things to see.
- <u>Romance</u> sometimes means wonder and adventure.

Manhattan

Morris Abel Beer

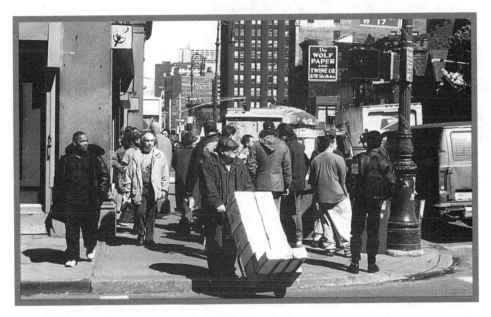

There's Asia on the avenue,
   And Europe in the street,
And Africa goes plodding by
   Beneath my window seat.

This is the wondrous city,
   Where worlds and nations meet;
Say not romance is napping;
   Behold the city street!

 Check-in
Which elements of poems—rhyme, rhythm, and repetition—helped you read and understand this poem? How do you think the speaker feels about Manhattan streets?

You've Got to Be Carefully Taught

Oscar Hammerstein

PHOTOFEST

You've got to be taught to hate and fear,
You've got to be taught from year to year,
It's got to be drummed in your dear little ear—
You've got to be carefully taught!

You've got to be taught to be afraid
Of people whose eyes are oddly made,
And people whose skin is a different shade—
You've got to be carefully taught.

You've got to be taught before it's too late,
Before you are six or seven or eight,
To hate all the people your relatives hate—
You've got to be carefully taught!
You've got to be carefully taught!

 Check-in
Which elements of poems—rhyme, rhythm, and repetition—
helped you read and understand the song? How do you think
the speaker feels about what he was saying?

After You Read

A. Did the Poems Make Sense? Reread sections you marked with a question mark (?). Do they make sense now? If not, discuss them with a partner or your instructor.

B. Build Your Vocabulary Look at the words you underlined. Can you figure them out now? If not, find out what they are. Add them to your word bank.

C. Answer These Questions

1. In which poem does the speaker celebrate the different races of people?

   _____

2. In which poem does the speaker sound angry about prejudice against people of different races?

   _____

3. Choose the message of "Manhattan."
   (1) Manhattan is full of people who are just alike.
   (2) Manhattan is a good place to find adventure and romance.
   (3) Manhattan is empty and boring.

4. Choose the message of "You've Got to Be Carefully Taught."
   (1) People are not born hating others; they are taught to hate.
   (2) People do not follow the things they are taught.
   (3) People who look different should be hated.

 Talk About It

Discuss the question below with a partner or small group.
If you like, write a response.

Why do you think some people teach their children to hate and fear people of other races and cultures?

Think About It: Identify Rhyme, Rhythm, and Repetition

You have learned three elements that poets use in writing poems. Some poems contain words that **rhyme.** Most poems have a **rhythm,** or a pattern of beats in the lines. And sometimes a poet will repeat a word or phrase. This **repetition** helps tell the message of the poem.

Practice Answer these questions about the two poems in this lesson.

1. Read the poem "Manhattan" aloud. Listen for the words that rhyme. Write the rhyming words.

   _____   _____

   _____   _____

2. Read the poem "You've Got to Be Carefully Taught" aloud. Listen for the words that rhyme. Write the three words in each group of rhyming words.

   _____   _____   _____

   _____   _____   _____

   _____   _____   _____

3. Read each poem aloud again. As you read, clap your hands together to the rhythm of the beat.

4. In "You've Got to Be Carefully Taught," what statement is repeated over and over?

   _____

5. On page 111, you chose the message of "You've Go to Be Carefully Taught." How does this repetition help tell the message?

   _____

Write About It: Write a Poem

You have read two poems about the differences among people. Now finish
a poem with your own ideas.

A. **Prewrite** On a separate piece of paper, write the headings **Different**
   and **Similar.** Think about how you are different from a person of
   another culture, race, or religion. Write down all your ideas under
   the **Different** heading. Then think of how you are like that other
   person. Write those ideas under the **Similar** heading.

B. **Write** Decide what feeling you want your poem to create. Decide if
   you want your poem to rhyme. Then choose your ideas that best fit
   the lines below and write them on the lines.

We Are Two People

We are different, you and I.

I am _____, but you are _____

I like _____, but you like _____

I _____, but you _____

We are different, you and I.

We are similar, you and I.

I am _____, and so are you.

You like _____, and so do I.

I _____, and you _____

We are similar, you and I.

▶ **Hold on to this work.** You may use it again at the end of this unit.

Writing Skills Mini-Lesson: Compound Sentences

You can combine two simple sentences into a **compound sentence** using the word *and* or *but*. For example,

Two simple sentences:
We come from many places. We have different cultures.

Compound sentence:
We come from many places, and we have different cultures.

Follow these rules.

1. Include a subject, a verb, and a complete thought in each part of the compound sentence.

        S V   S V

    We come from many places, and **we have** different customs.

2. The word *and* connects two related ideas. The word *but* connects two contrasting ideas. Use a comma (,) before *and* or *but*.

    We come from many places, **and** we have different customs.

    Our customs are different, **but** we have many things in common.

Practice On your own paper, combine these simple sentences to make compound sentences. Use *and* or *but* correctly. The first one is done as an example.

1. My building is large. Many different people live there.

    <u>My building is large, and many different people live there.</u>

2. The Parks are from Korea. They sometimes cook Korean food for me.

3. The Ortegas do not speak English at home. They speak English with their neighbors.

4. We are different in many ways. We still like each other.

Unit 4 Review

Reading Review

This reading is about encountering different cultures. Read it and then answer the questions.

In a Strange City

Maria was a little scared. She and her older brother, Carlos, had just stepped off the bus. They had come to live in a strange city in a different country. Maria hoped they would be able to find the home of their aunt and uncle.

"Don't look so worried, little one," Carlos said. Maria was 18, but he still called her little one. "Aunt Gloria said to take Bus 165 west on Adams Street. When we get to 35th Street, we'll get off the bus. We can call from the corner."

Carlos stopped a woman and asked the way to Adams Street. It was just a block away. A short while later, the two were on the bus. Maria looked out the window to see her new home. She could read a little English, but she could not read the signs she saw. She began to look worried. Carlos told her they were in a neighborhood where people from Europe lived. He thought the signs might be Polish.

A few blocks later, the signs changed. She could not read them at all. She looked even more worried. "It's a Chinese neighborhood," Carlos told her.

"I'll never get around in this city," Maria thought to herself.

Then Maria saw a sign she could easily read. It was in both English and Spanish. She saw another, and another. "Here we are!" Carlos cried happily as the bus stopped at 35th Street. "Our new neighborhood."

Maria smiled happily, too. She was no longer so worried about her decision to come to this new city. In fact, Maria decided to do something else. When she got to know her new neighborhood, she would go back to the other neighborhoods she had passed and learn about them, too.

1. What is Maria's problem in the story?
   (1) She is lost with her older brother.
   (2) She missed the bus to her aunt and uncle's house.
   (3) She is scared of being in a new city and country.

2. What kind of person does Carlos seem to be?
   (1) tense and worried
   (2) able to take care of things
   (3) funny and light-hearted

3. Which country do you think Maria and Carlos are from?
   (1) Mexico
   (2) Poland
   (3) China

Writing Process

In Unit 4, you wrote three first drafts. Choose the piece that you would like to work with more. Then revise, edit, and make a final copy of it.

_____ your description of your favorite holiday (page 98)
_____ your autobiography (page 106)
_____ your poem (page 113)

Find the first draft you chose. Then turn to page 128 in this book. Follow steps 3, 4, and 5 in the Writing Process to create a final draft.

As you revise, check your draft for this specific point:

Description: Did you include clear details about your holiday?
Autobiography: Did you tell facts that are usually found in an autobiography?
Poem: Does your poem get your feelings across?

▶ Skills Review

This review will let you see how well you can use the skills covered in this book. When you have completed Units 1–4, do this review. Then share your work with your instructor.

Reading Skills

Read the poem and the biography. Then choose the best answer to each question.

Husbands and Wives

Miriam Hershenson

Husbands and wives
    With children between them
Sit in the subway;
    So I have seen them.

One word only
    From station to station;
So much talk for
    So close a relation.

1. A word in the poem that rhymes with the word *station* is
   (1) subway
   (2) relation
   (3) children
2. What do the lines "One word only / From station to station" mean?
   (1) A man called out the name of each station before the subway stopped there.
   (2) Husbands and wives barely spoke as the subway moved along.
   (3) Angry people do not talk to each other.
3. What is the main message the speaker in the poem is trying to tell?
   (1) It is hard to talk when you have children sitting between you.
   (2) Watching people as you ride the subway can be interesting.
   (3) Married couples sometimes don't need to say many words in order to communicate.

From Cuba to Success in the United States

Gloria Estefan was born in Cuba. Her family moved to the United States when she was 16 years old. Gloria loved to sing. She worked hard on a singing career. Her hard work paid off. In time, she began to have hit song after hit song.

Then Gloria was hurt when her tour bus crashed. Her back was broken. Doctors were able to help fix her back. But it took one year of hard work for Gloria to heal fully.

Gloria has worked hard to help Cuban Americans. Miami, Florida, is home to many Cuban Americans. After a hurricane hit Florida, she gave concerts to raise money. The money was given to Cuban Americans who had been hurt by the storm. Gloria is proud to be a Cuban American. The people of Miami are proud of Gloria.

4. Which of the following tells the main idea of the biography?
   (1) Gloria Estefan has worked hard for herself and for Cuban Americans.
   (2) Gloria Estefan is a Cuban American singer with many hits.
   (3) Gloria Estefan was born in Cuba but moved to the United States.

5. How has Gloria helped the people who live in Miami?
   (1) She tells them she is proud of them.
   (2) She helped raise money after a hurricane.
   (3) She is proud to be a Cuban American.

6. What can you infer from the statement "But it took one year of hard work for Gloria to heal fully"?
   (1) Gloria did not take care of herself.
   (2) Gloria had been badly hurt.
   (3) The doctors did not do a good job.

Writing Skills

A. On a separate paper add the endings and write the new words.

1. family + es
2. go + ing
3. hope + ed
4. hid + en
5. celebrate + ing

6. excite + able
7. hop + ing
8. chew + able
9. bit + en
10. dry + ing

11. wed + ing
12. serve + ice
13. apply + ed
14. rehearse + al
15. amaze + ing

16. ship + ment
17. stop + er
18. funny + er
19. vary + ous
20. exist + ence

B. On a separate paper, combine the simple sentences to make compound sentences.

1. My family likes food from different countries. I try to surprise them with new recipes.
2. We like to go to restaurants. We can't afford to eat out often.
3. We all like Greek food. There is a good Greek restaurant nearby.
4. My husband likes Middle Eastern food. Some of it doesn't agree with him.

C. On a separate paper, copy the paragraph below. Correct any mistakes you find in spelling, capitalization, or punctuation.

my son calvin and his two boys lived with me for three years. I watchd my grandbabys when calvin workked. I loved to be with Ben and Marcus and they loved to be with me. then Calvin got marryed to tina in june.

i was happy about this but there was a down side. Calvin and tina moved to memphis. i don't see them very much. I miss my grandbabies

I am planing to see them this fall I am hopping that they will come to my house for thanksgiving. I can hardly wait

Write About It

On a separate paper, write about the topic below. Follow steps 1–5 of the Writing Process on page 128. Make changes on your draft to improve your writing. Then share your revised draft with your instructor.

Topic: What does the word *family* mean to you? What makes a family?

Skills Review Answers

Reading Skills

1. (2) **4.** (1)

2. (2) **5.** (2)

3. (3) **6.** (2)

Writing Skills

A.
1. families	**6.** excitable	**11.** wedding	**16.** shipment
2. going	**7.** hopping	**12.** service	**17.** stopper
3. hoped	**8.** chewable	**13.** applied	**18.** funnier
4. hidden	**9.** bitten	**14.** rehearsal	**19.** various
5. celebrating	**10.** drying	**15.** amazing	**20.** existence

B.
1. My family likes food from different countries, and I try to surprise them with new recipes.
2. We like to go to restaurants, but we can't afford to eat out often.
3. We all like Greek food, and there is a good Greek restaurant nearby.
4. My husband likes Middle Eastern food, but some of it doesn't agree with him.

C. Compare your paragraph to the corrected version.

My son Calvin and his two boys lived with me for three years. I watched my grandbabies when Calvin worked. I loved to be with Ben and Marcus, and they loved to be with me. Then Calvin got married to Tina in June.

I was happy about this, but there was a down side. Calvin and Tina moved to Memphis. I don't see them very much. I miss my grandbabies.

I am planning to see them this fall. I am hoping that they will come to my house for Thanksgiving. I can hardly wait.

Evaluation Chart

Check your Reading Skills answers. Then circle the number of any answer you missed on the chart below. You may need to review the lesson pages indicated next to that question number.

Question	Skill	Lessons
1	identify rhyme	3, 12
2	make inferences	6, 7, 9, 11
3	understand main idea	2, 8
4	understand main idea	2, 8
5	find details	2, 8
6	make inferences	6, 7, 9, 11

▶ **Now go back** and fill in the right side of the Student Interest Inventory on page 6.

Answer Key

▼ Lesson 1

After You Read (p. 17)
C. 1. a. Any of these: worried, scared, alone, tense
      b. Any of these: happy, relieved
   2. (2)
   3. (1)

Think About It: Understand Plot (p. 18)
Practice
Possible answers:
Rising action: Marla is sick and worried.
Climax: Marla's mother, Ann, comes.
Falling action: Ann says she will help Marla.

Write About It: Write a Sequence of Events (p. 20)
A. Order of events listed: 4, 1, 3, 5, 2

Word Work: The Vowel Combinations *ie* and *ei* (p. 21)
C. 1. tie
   2. receipt
   3. sleigh
   4. niece
   5. leisure

▼ Lesson 2

After You Read (p. 25)
C. 1. why he is in prison, what life in prison is like, how his being in prison was not his son's fault, what he wants his son to do
   2. (2)
   3. Possible answers: He loves him. He cares very much about him.

Think About It: Understand the Main Idea and Details (p. 26)
Practice
1. (2)
2. Main idea: Fred has plans to spend the day with his son.
   Details should include: (1) a bike ride, (2) lunch, (3) a ball game, (4) a movie

Word Work: The Letter Combinations *ow* and *ou* (p. 29)
C. 1. now
   2. mow
   3. though
   4. mouth
   5. touch

▼ Lesson 3

After You Read (p. 32)
C. 2. (2)
   3. (1)

Think About It: Identify Rhythm and Rhyme (p. 33)
Practice
A. 1. cried
   2. weigh
   3. allow
   4. shown
   5. about
   6. though
B. There are many possible answers. Check yours with your instructor.

▼ Writing Skills Mini-Lesson: Adding Endings that Start with a Vowel (p. 36)
Practice
Last night, my family was **relaxing** and **playing** cards with my two aunts. Suddenly my **older** aunt **announced**, "Luis and I are **getting married**." My mother **hugged** her, **crying**, "Finally! I never **stopped hoping**. You'll be the **happiest** couple." Then all of us **started planning** the wedding.

▼ Unit 1 Review (p. 37)
Reading Review
1. (1)
2. (2)
3. (1)

▼ Lesson 4

After You Read (p. 43)
C. 1. (2)
   2. (2)
   3. (1)

Think About It: Understand Character (p. 44)

Practice

1. Possible answers: quiet, lives alone, feels alone, doesn't show her feelings, cares about Carmen, young, short black hair, large eyes
3. (1)
4. Possible answers: young, enjoy each other's company
5. Possible answers: Rosa is quiet; Carmen likes people. Rosa is alone; Carmen is married with a son.

Word Work: Context Clues (p. 47)

Practice

1. cafeteria
2. bothered
3. mirror

▼ **Lesson 5**

After You Read (p. 50)

C. 1. Possible answers: sad, depressed, down, in shock
   3. (2)
   4. (2)

Think About It: Understand the Use of Repetition (p. 51)

Practice

1. From tomorrow on
2. being sad
3. No, because tomorrow never comes. It becomes today.
4. (2)

▼ **Lesson 6**

After You Read (p. 57)

C. 1. There are many possible answers. Here are three: He was born with health problems. He is deaf. He lives on his own now.
   2. Possible answers:
      a. His parents helped him look for an apartment.
      b. He had a hearing-ear dog.
      c. He has a TTY.
   3. (1)

Think About It: Make Inferences (p. 58)

Practice

1. yes

2. (1)
3. (2)

Word Work: Context Clues (p. 61)

Practice

1. (1)
2. (2)
3. (2)
4. (1)

▼ **Writing Skills Mini-Lesson: Using Capital Letters (p. 62)**

Practice

One Tuesday last November, there was a terrible fire in Springfield. It burned our building and two others to the ground. My wife and I lost everything. Our neighbor, Evelyn Williams, let us stay with her. That week, Ms. Williams gave us clothes and even made us Thanksgiving dinner. She also helped us find a new apartment. In December, my family and I invited her to celebrate Kwanzaa in our new home.

▼ **Unit 2 Review (p. 63)**

Reading Review

1. (2)
2. (1)
3. (2)

Unit 3 New Beginnings

▼ **Lesson 7**

After You Read (p. 69)

C. 1. (2)
   2. (1)
   3. (2)
   4. (2)

Think About It: Make Inferences (p. 70)

Practice

1. (1)
2. (2)
3. (1)

▼ **Lesson 8**

After You Read (p. 75)

C. 1. (3)
   2. (1)

3. Possible answers: how to help his daughters, how to deal with the hurt he felt, suggestions for how to meet new people

Think About It: Understand the Main Idea and Details (p. 76)
Practice

A. 1. (3)
   2. Possible answers:
   - They do not understand.
   - Jane thinks I am angry with her.
   - But she is still upset.
   - Amy is having a hard time too.
   - Last night on the phone, she asked, "When are we coming home, Daddy?"

B. 1. Some couples marry too young.
   2. Some couples do not talk enough.
   3. Sometimes couples grow apart.

Word Work: Compound Words (p. 79)

A. 1. a. after/noon, after, noon
       b. suit/cases, suit, cases
       c. drive/way, drive, way
   2. Possible answers: without, another, anyone, understand, daydream, upset, maybe

B. 1. sun/screen, pay/check
   2. back/yard, bath/tub, news/stand, worried
   3. door/way, meeting, hair/cut, peace/maker

▼ Lesson 9
After You Read (p. 83)

C. 1. Here are three possible answers: She was born in China. She came to the United States. She ran a successful laundry with her family.
   2. proud, hard-working, down-to-earth
   3. Possible answer: will succeed because she works hard to get what she wants

Think About It: Make Inferences (p. 84)
Practice

1. yes   4. no
2. no   5. yes
3. yes   6. yes

Word Work: Prefixes and Roots (p. 87)

A. 1. unusual
   2. antidrug

3. replay
4. unkind
5. rebuild
6. unsure
7. antifreeze
8. reproduce

B. 1. re/read
   2. anti/social
   3. un/pleasant
   4. re/fuel
   5. anti/septic
   6. un/familiar
   7. un/necessary
   8. re/arrange

▼ Writing Skills Mini-Lesson: Writing Sentences (p. 88)
Practice

There are different ways to rewrite the sentences correctly. Here are some possible answers:

1. **I want to** improve my reading and writing **skills.**
2. Recently, **I went** back to school.
3. **I am preparing for** a good career.
4. What are **you** going to study**?**
5. I am interested in **computers.**

▼ Unit 3 Review (p. 89)
Reading Review

1. (1)
2. (3)
3. (3)

Unit 4 Celebrate Differences

▼ Lesson 10
After You Read (p. 95)

C. Possible answers:
   1. Your answers will depend on the way you celebrate your holiday.
   2. He had no one to spend Christmas with.
   3. He began to talk to the Kahns. He invited his neighbors into his apartment. He made new friends.
   4. Brenda has an idea. Brenda invites everyone to their apartment to share special food and customs.

Think About It: Understand Plot and Character (p. 96)
Practice
1. (1)
2. (3)
3. (2)
4. **Rising action:** No one will have a traditional holiday.
   Climax: Brenda says, "Let's celebrate together!"
   Falling action: They all agree to celebrate together.
5. Paul Black, Brenda Kahn, Barry Kahn, Wanda Mays
6. Possible answers: young, alone, lonely, friendly, outgoing, homesick

Word Work: Suffixes -ful, -less, -able, -or (p. 99)
A. 1. creator
   2. helpless
   3. dependable
   4. successful
   5. useful
   6. adorable
   7. careless
   8. counselor
B. 1. sorrow/ful
   2. breath/less
   3. agree/able
   4. spectat/or
   5. profit/able
   6. thought/ful
   7. use/less
   8. act/or

▼ **Lesson 11**
After You Read (p. 103)
C. 1. where he was born, when he was born, what his childhood was like, what he does for a living
   2. (1)
   3. Possible answers: loyal, hard-working, Japanese American, patriotic, successful, served his country

Think About It: Make Inferences (p. 104)
Practice
1. Yes
2. No
3. Yes
4. Yes

Word Work: The Suffix -ion (p. 107)
A. 1. direction
   2. discussion
   3. confusion
   4. reaction
   5. location
   6. inspection
B. 1. adopt + ion
   2. celebrate + ion
   3. complete + ion
C. Check your answers with your instructor.

▼ **Lesson 12**
After You Read (p. 111)
C. 1. "Manhattan"
   2. "You've Got to Be Carefully Taught"
   3. (2)
   4. (1)

Think About It: Identify Rhyme, Rhythm, and Repetition (p. 112)
Practice
1. street, seat, meet, street
2. fear, year, ear
   afraid, made, shade
   late, eight, hate
4. "You've got to be taught." *or* "You've got to be carefully taught."
5. Possible answer: It helps stress that hate is learned.

▼ **Writing Skills Mini-Lesson: Compound Sentences (p. 114)**
Practice
2. The Parks are from Korea, and they sometimes cook Korean food for me.
3. The Ortegas do not speak English at home, but they speak English with their neighbors.
4. We are different in many ways, but we still like each other.

▼ **Unit 4 Review (p. 115)**
Reading Review
1. (3)
2. (2)
3. (1)

Writing Skills

This handbook lists the rules you learned in the Writing Skills Mini-Lessons in this book.

Spelling Rules: Adding Endings that Start with a Vowel

1. **For most words, just add the ending.**

   look + ing = looking   play + er = player   assist + ant = assistant

2. **If a one-syllable word ends with one vowel and one consonant, double the final consonant (unless it is *w* or *x*).**

   drop + ed = dropped   hid + en = hidden   **but:** fix + ed = fixed

3. **If a word ends with a silent *e*, drop the *e*.**

   type + ist = typist   use + able = usable   operate + or = operator

4. **If a word ends with a consonant plus *y*, change the *y* to *i* unless the ending starts with *i*.**

   happy + est = happiest   carry + er = carrier   **but:** carry + ing = carrying

Rules for Using Capital Letters

1. **Capitalize the first word of a sentence and the word *I*.**

   There was a fire last year. My wife and **I** lost everything.

2. **Capitalize the days of the week, holidays, and months.**

   Monday, Friday, Labor Day, Thanksgiving Day, January, May

3. **Capitalize the names of places (cities, states, countries, continents).**

   St. Louis, California, Mexico, Asia

4. **Capitalize people's names and titles.**

   David Gelman, the Hassans, Dr. Julia Estevez

Writing Complete Sentences

To write a correct, complete **sentence,** follow these rules:

1. **Write a complete thought.**

    Not complete: To prepare for a career.

    Complete: I am taking classes to prepare for a career.

2. **Include a subject (telling who or what the sentence is about) and a verb (telling what the subject does or is).**

    S   V
    This **school offers** computer courses.

    S V
    I am a student in this school.

    S   V
    I have taken many classes here.

    S   V
    The **instructor** in room 104 **teaches** well.

3. **Start with a capital letter and end with a period (.), question mark (?), or exclamation point (!).**

    It is ten o'clock**.** Where were you**?** You missed the exam**!**

Writing Compound Sentences

You can combine two simple sentences into a **compound sentence** using the word *and* or *but*. Follow these rules.

1. **Include a subject, a verb, and a complete thought in each part of the compound sentence.**

    S V   S V
    We come from many places, and **we have** different customs.

2. **The word *and* connects two related ideas. The word *but* connects two contrasting ideas. Use a comma (,) before *and* or *but*.**

    We come from many places**, and** we have different customs.

    Our customs are different**, but** we have many things in common.

The Writing Process

The Writing Process is a series of stages that can help you create a good piece of writing. These stages are shown below.

1. Prewrite, or plan your writing. _____

A. Think about your topic.

B. List ideas about your topic.

C. Organize your ideas.
- Decide which ideas you will use.
- Decide how you will order them.

2. Write a first draft. _____

A. Use your ideas from stage 1.

B. Write about your topic.
- Include your most important ideas.
- Use details to explain what you mean.

3. Revise your first draft. _____

A. Check that your draft

____ includes your important ideas

____ has details to explain what you mean

____ is clear and easy to understand

B. Make changes to improve your writing.

4. Edit your work. _____

A. Check your draft for errors in

____ spelling

____ punctuation

____ capitalization

B. Correct any mistakes you find. If you need help, use the Writing Skills Handbook on page 126 or ask your instructor.

5. Recopy your draft. _____

A. Write a final draft. Include all of your revising and editing changes.

B. Compare your first and final drafts. Note improvements.

C. Share your final draft with a classmate, a friend, or your instructor.